Spiritual

CROSS-TRAINING

SEARCHING THROUGH SILENCE, STRETCH, AND SONG

BENJAMIN SHALVA

PRESS

AUTHOR'S NOTE: The stories in this book were composed from memory without additional research, and the names and identities of the characters have been altered to protect privacy.

Published by Grand Harbor Press, Grand Haven.

www.brilliancepublishing.com

Amazon, the Amazon logo, and Grand Harbor Press are trademarks of Amazon.com, Inc., or its affiliates.

ISBN-13: 9781503950481
ISBN-10: 1503950484

Cover design by Jeff Miller, Faceout Studio

Printed in the United States of America

Spiritual

CROSS-
TRAINING

For Sara,
my teacher, lover, and best friend

TABLE OF CONTENTS

Like
A pair
Of mismatched newlyweds,
One of whom still feels very insecure,
I keep turning to God
Saying,
"Kiss
Me."

— *Hafiz*

INVITATION

Cross-training. We've heard of this before—a sequence of exercises that engage our many and varied muscle groups. But *spiritual* cross-training? Really? What is that?

The word *spiritual* carries many different connotations. Some of us hear "spiritual" and think of God, in whole or in part, named or unnamed, detailed in Scripture or imagined in moments of wonder and awe. Others link "spiritual" with concepts like the Source of Life, the Universal One, Goodness, Higher Power, Higher Consciousness, Humanistic Altruism or the humble pursuit of an ethical, meaningful, value-filled Life.

For our purposes, any or all of these definitions will do. Spiritual cross-training, like its physical analogue, is the search for God (or Soul or Goodness or Fill-in-the-Blank) through the engagement of our many and varied *spiritual* muscle groups.

For some, organized religious traditions will provide a key component of this training. For others, religious affiliation may not be essential. When I cross-train, I follow traditional paths of silence, stretch, and song, practicing established lineages of meditation, yoga, and prayer. Your cross-training regimen may provide the same nourishment through very different means. Perhaps your cross-training takes you not to the meditation cushion but to the hiking trail. When you stretch, maybe you do so not on a yoga mat but on a surfboard, undulating with the waves.

In this book, I present to you my story—one man's search through silence, stretch, and song. I offer these words with the understanding that my journey will not be yours. Your spiritual cross-training may include the three modalities of silence, stretch, and song—or only some of them. You may envision other means to climb the mountain, walking paths I've yet to discover.

As you turn these pages, I only ask of you what I ask of myself. Search with an open mind and a light heart. Be willing to try something new. Train with me for a while, flexing our spiritual muscles in tandem as we move up the mountain. Walk with me, searching for the summit together. Then, if you need to break away and head up a different path, no big deal. I know we'll see each other again. I know, before too long, our paths will cross. And when they do, we'll have wonderful stories to share.

INTRODUCTION

I have been searching all my life. My search began in the meditation hall, moved to the synagogue and traveled again to the yoga mat. Along the way, I searched in the mountains of Tibet and in the alleyways of Jerusalem, at the keys of the piano and on the theatrical stage. I saw therapists. I took psychedelics and antidepressants. I studied the Bible. I wept and laughed and prayed. I fell in love, married and fathered two children. I ministered as a rabbi to congregations, universities, summer camps and prisons. I have never stopped searching.

After more than ten thousand hours of this spiritual search, I learned that it produces nothing tangible.

Imagine searching for the wind—you walk out to the open field. You wait. You hear something in the distance. Suddenly, you feel it, the tender wind on your cheek. "I've found it!" you exclaim. Your friends and family come running. They've waited so patiently. They gather around you, first excited, then confused. What have you found? Your hands remain empty. You hold nothing but stories.

We who search—what do we really have to offer? Hands empty, we tell our stories.

When I began to tell my stories to family, friends, colleagues and congregants—stories that traversed so many spiritual arenas, stories that, more often than not, ended in a bewildering blend of revelation and regret—I awaited rebuke. I imagined others would shake their heads, wag their fingers, and scold me for playing the field. "Why did you need to explore?" I expected to hear. "Why couldn't you content yourself with one religious tradition, one spiritual path?"

Instead of admonishment, I received encouragement. And the request, again and again, to share what I'd learned. While I was busy castigating myself for a lack of religious fidelity, others were thanking me for outfitting my toolbox with such a diverse assortment of techniques. A congregant, whose husband had left her for another woman, thanked me for helping her traverse those turbulent waters with the help of meditation. A corporation invited me into the stratosphere of their high-rise, glass-walled offices to teach their executives how to stretch. A summer camp welcomed me to their wooded enclave to lead campers and staff in embodied song.

With my face pressed close against my own life's canvas, I saw an amorphous mess of haphazard brushstrokes. When I stepped back, a very different painting emerged. A new story began to unfold. I hadn't been dabbling. I'd been *cross-training*.

Without intending to, I'd bounded back and forth between three arenas of spiritual practice: *silence, stretch, and song*. These three distinct paths had collectively moved me up the mountain. Together, silence, stretch, and song had propelled me to new spiritual heights.

Why silence, stretch, and song? Why had I gravitated to these three modes of worship? While each path presented a unique set of challenges, exercising different spiritual muscle groups, a common thread ran through them all—body and breath. When I studied holy texts, though I found this enriching, the wisdom usually stayed in my head. Silence, stretch, and song invited me to actualize my search for God, turning it from theoretical aspiration to embodied action.

Rumi, the thirteenth-century Sufi poet, writes, "Don't open the door to the study and begin reading. Take down a musical instrument. Let the beauty we love be what we do. There are hundreds of ways to kneel and kiss the ground." How do I bring worship alive? By taking down the instrument, the yoga mat, the meditation cushion. By moving worship into every cell of my body.

I hadn't intended to cross-train. I began this journey with the intention to master one spiritual modality. For years at a time, I focused exclusively on a single practice, calling it my own, claiming it as my chosen tradition. I grew accustomed to that familiar feeling of a meditation cushion under my tush, a mat beneath my feet or a prayer book in my hands. Patting myself on the back, I declared, "I meditate" or "I sing and dance and pray." Unintentionally, I turned each chosen path into a lovely, rewarding, *safe* hobby. Contemplative practice provided comfort and security, chicken soup for my lonely, ravaged soul.

But the God I was searching for was not a God copyrighted and distributed by one religion, philosophy or creed, but the God of pre-rational, resonant, revelatory awe. The God of soft hearts and open eyes. The God of vulnerability, honesty, presence, and courage. To train for such high altitudes, spiritual practice needed to hurt a little. Enough to clutter complacency. Enough to get me feeling like a child again, a beginner, inquisitive, even suspicious. Better the insecurity of wonder than decided, determined and dull.

My yoga teacher, Tony Sanchez, went into retreat for a decade, practicing yoga all day, every day. He emerged to tell us that we would all do well to augment our yoga practice with cooking classes. In other words, dear yogis, we can ease up a bit and delight in life. But how can we delight if we're stubbornly ambitious, if we're settled upon one path alone?

Love softens the heart by virtue of its irrationality. We fall in love, go crazy, and that's how we grow. To grow close to God, to fall in love with my soul within and my world without, I needed to release my agenda, to allow each spiritual path to wind toward absurdity. I needed to edge my way to the cliff, stare into the abyss and mutter, *This is insane.* At that moment, my spiritual practice would transform from lovely hobby to life-altering pilgrimage. From that vantage point, I could look back at the terrain I'd covered and finally understand—*we* don't meditate. *God breathes us. We* don't practice yoga. *God stretches us. We* don't sing. *God lifts us in song.*

So, I took three paths up the mountain, immersing myself in silence, stretch, and song. I avoided any single ascent. I let one practice go for a time while I focused on the other two. I stopped meditating while still stretching and singing. Then, when the time felt right, I tried meditation again. No big deal. I stopped singing. Then a synagogue offered me a job singing on Sunday mornings with its Hebrew school students. I took the job, wishing all the while that I could spend the hours teaching yoga instead. But the job blew my heart wide open. Those Sunday mornings of song made my yoga practice lighter and deeper.

After decades of walking the spiritual path, of oscillating between silence, stretch, and song, I'm still surprised each time my work on one path elevates my work on another. That's the ingredient that will help us on the path to God. Surprise. Spiritual practice works when it blows our mind. So mix it up, let it unsettle you to your core. Take three paths and braid them unskillfully. This isn't dabbling. It's cross-training.

To introduce myself to silence, stretch, and song, to familiarize myself with each path's choreography, I studied with experienced teachers—spiritual coaches who had spent their lives exploring this terrain. One coach taught me how to weave my voice together with others in song. Another coach helped me ease into a back bend safely. Each coach shared stories from the road. These stories reassured and inspired.

And the very best coaches, they always stopped me as I ambitiously charged out the door. I couldn't wait to get home and practice what I'd learned, but these teachers would slow me down with a twinkle in their eye and a sly little smile. "Don't take any of this too seriously," they would whisper. The best coaches were the ones who knew how to laugh.

Eventually, at the heart of the search, I became my own coach. I noticed things I'd never noticed before. I fell down a lot, yes, but I got up, too. I started to know gratitude and grace in my bones. This was the time for me to write my own stories, to get to know my own laughter's unique cadence. This was also my opportunity to support others on the path, to witness a deeper current that carries all of our lonely searches toward the same shore.

And so, this book was born.

In these pages, I will serve as a spiritual cross-training coach and fellow seeker. In my capacity as coach, I will offer techniques, tell stories, and try to *shlep* a little joy. As a fellow seeker, I will pour my yearning into these pages. I will open myself to you. When I picture you, my reader, I picture a friend. May these words help us both feel alive and full of wonder. May this journey help us all feel less alone.

PART I:

SILENCE

THE VALLEY OF WORDS

We spend our days awash in words. Words are the air we breathe. Cell phones give us conversations during even our most isolated moments. Computer screens illuminate an eternal stream of words, our fingers replying even as our mouths enjoy a rare respite. We don't have to condemn our verbosity. This is just the human way. Even in the Judeo-Christian story of creation, God constructs the universe with words. *God said: Let there be light, and there was light* (Gen. 1:3). We can love the word, delighting in something we've just read, leaning in close over a drink to get something off our chest. We can love the word.

For many of us, silence feels incredibly uncomfortable. We find ourselves alone, in a quiet spot. We sit down, or remain standing, or walk around. We're not talking. We're not listening to anyone else speak. We're not reading or writing. Maybe we're outside and it's a pretty day. Sunshine might be exactly what we thought we wanted—a beautiful, peaceful place to just be for a while, outside in the sun. Yet, after a few minutes, or even a few seconds, we start to feel itchy, edgy. Why? It's just a little break. Why can't we sit still and enjoy it? In a world of noise, why does silence feel so arduous?

We experience symptoms of withdrawal in the midst of silence because, whether we admit it or not, we're addicted to words. The vehicle for the very creation of the universe has become a compulsion. After all, here we sit in a peaceful, quiet setting. No one's abusing us. We're not performing some great ascetic feat. Yet we can't wait to go, to get back to our words, to leave the meadow, to call someone we love and talk their ear off.

Our addiction to words, our discomfort with silence, has everything to do with what we don't want to see. I first discovered this while attending a college study-abroad program in Tibetan studies. Our semester began in Dharamsala, India, the de facto capital of Tibet's diaspora, then continued in Kathmandu, another center for Tibetans in exile, and concluded with a month in Tibet.

Dharamsala delighted. Kathmandu enticed. Tibet took the senses and stripped them bare. Tibet was a four-hundred-and-sixty-thousand-square-mile tabula rasa, a wild west with honest-to-God tumbleweeds rolling through the middle of even the busiest streets. On those same streets, Tibetan natives and Chinese immigrants shuffled here and there quietly, stifled, I imagined, as much by the horizonless expanse as China's totalitarian occupation.

Following a few days of touring in Lhasa, we students piled into a cavalcade of Land Rovers and headed for the mountains. Tibetan porters joined our group as we toured by car. At every stop, they set up a mess tent and cooked our meals. Our program directors had warned us that a few of these porters worked as spies for the Chinese government. Discussions of Chinese-Tibetan politics would need to wait until we returned to Kathmandu.

So began a three-week journey across southern Tibet. We'd bounce along for hours in our Land Rovers, listening to mix tapes to pass the time, stopping to visit isolated villages and abandoned monasteries every few hours. More often than not, when our caravan would halt, we'd emerge from our vehicles in the middle of absolutely nowhere. No buildings. No traffic. No vegetation. No people. Occasionally, a yak or two in the distance.

During one of these pit stops, I caught movement on some low hills a few hundred yards away. A few minutes more, and I realized I was watching a half-dozen Tibetan children, no older than six or seven, walking in our direction. Where they had come from, I don't know. They soon sidled up to our caravan, dressed in traditional Tibetan garb, faces ruddy, noses running, smiling so sweetly that we emptied our pockets of all candy and sent them running back to the hills, laughing in delight.

On one evening in particular, after spending the day climbing up a steep mountainside, our group reached an abandoned monastery nestled upon a plateau midway up the mountain. Even with porters shouldering most of our provisions, the long climb in thin air had exhausted us. A bunch of guys, myself included, threw our sleeping bags into one of the monastery's empty buildings. Then, with nothing better to do before dinner, we began to entertain ourselves with a testosterone-fueled chorus of crude jokes and playful insults.

I remember vividly how one member of our boys club refrained from participating in our playful banter. John, silent as always, sat nearby, listening without expression. John made me nervous. He stood a foot taller and a thousand words quieter than the rest of us. When he did speak, John's words strolled their way from his tongue soft and slow, unconcerned whether they reached an ear or fell to the floor.

John served as our program's resident pothead. Any time we arrived to a new locale, he located the hash. This search proved easiest in the tourist neighborhoods of Kathmandu, where a few American dollars could buy enough hash to last well beyond one's travel visa. John appeared to have spent this entire semester blazed and blurry. I felt sorry for him. I enjoyed getting high the way I enjoyed going to the movies; when the movie ended, you went back to your life. You didn't order another bucket of popcorn, unroll a sleeping bag and make your home in the theater. I looked at John and imagined a suffering soul locked behind that prison of smoke, his quiet demeanor just another symptom of a campaign of avoidance and repression.

In addition to feeling sorry for John, I just didn't understand him. I grew up in a family of talkers. Proudly verbose, I processed the world with words. Quiet people unnerved me. What were they waiting for? Why didn't they speak? Did they think they were better than us? Or were they, like the great prophet Moses during his humble beginnings, "slow of speech and tongue," unfortunate incompetents in our great verbal age?

Not that I enjoyed this makeshift locker room we'd created that first evening in the monastery. Having been on the receiving end of all-male hazing when it devolved from playful to punishing, I hoped this flurry of benign teasing would soon run its course. I felt sorry for John, but I envied him, too. There he sat, vibrating on a different frequency than the rest of us, immune to the verbal exchange I secretly loathed but nevertheless helped to create. A silent stoner I wasn't, but at that moment, I would have gladly switched places with him. I had begun to suffocate from all these words.

Envy emboldened me. If John wouldn't come to the party, the party would have to come to him. Following a witty repartee among a few of our peers, I turned to John and said with a giddy grin, "So, John, are you quiet because you have things to say and you don't say them, or are you quiet because you just have nothing to say?" Everyone fell silent. John looked at me and slowly replied, "If I have something to say, I'll say it."

More silence. Then another member of our group said, "Ben, shut the fuck up." Some chuckles. And that was that. The others moved on.

The banter continued. I stayed there for a few minutes more, ashamed but intimating that I had moved on from the uncomfortable exchange. Then I exited the building into the quickly darkening twilight.

I began to walk, following a narrow, rocky path that led out from the monastery grounds. The path dipped down and then around a bend, ending at a magnificent waterfall. I sat down. The water rushed white in front of me, spilling from high above and cascading to far below. Its roar offered a welcome wall of sound, dispelling Tibet's oppressive silence.

Then, coming into focus against the twilight backdrop, I saw them. Strange, colorful projections swirling around me. One burst into focus and then faded, immediately replaced by the next. Here—the face of my father enraged. There—a childhood memory grown wings and a tail.

These countless demons leaped and danced, each one passing before my eyes. I had never before seen them, never witnessed their dance, yet I knew in my bones that they had been with me for a very, very long time. They were wild and frightening and they were mine.

As they danced, I saw with absolute clarity that virtually everything I said, every word I spoke, came from these demons. Minute by minute, day by day, year by year, they poked me in the ribs, sank their nails deep into my shoulders, stirred my guts, and I, under attack, had been calling out with two decades' worth of carefully constructed persona, working to make it okay with every word. But it was not okay. My demons lived and breathed and made me sick without me doing a damn thing about it; I was too busy pretending they weren't there, buoying myself with so many words, babbling enough to distract myself, to ease my pain.

As I watched these demons dance, I recognized how helpless I was to exorcise them. They lurked deep in my psyche, nestled in memory, invisible and inaccessible to my waking mind. I could strike at them, but in my untrained clumsiness I would most likely miss, injuring the best of me with each blow.

No, conventional warfare would not do. Non-violent protest, on the other hand, a concerted campaign of disengagement—that might disturb their cozy habitation. So right then and there, I made a decision. I would not wrestle my demons, but neither would I respond to their provocations. Let them agitate, let them whisper ancient worries, let the anxiety come. I would no longer react. I would just stop listening.

The place to launch my liberation was the word. In the past, when inner demons tickled and teased, I vomited great geysers of words, words I didn't mean, words I didn't even understand. I chattered and babbled, the sound of my own voice sedating me enough to feel the fear yet function within a spectrum of normalcy. While I couldn't stop the demons, I could stop the words. My tongue was my own. What if, like John, I spoke when and only when I honestly had something to say? It might not end the anxiety, but at least my actions, my interface with others, my very voice—these would belong to me.

I stood up. The waterfall roared. It had provided a gift, a vision, a brief peek behind the curtain. Now the work began.

The following morning, I entered the breakfast tent to warm up with a cup of yak's milk tea. Another equally groggy participant came up to me and said, "Good morning." I answered back, "Good morning." Sure enough, I felt a little tickle, a little tug from my gut: *Say something. Make conversation. She'll think you're weird. Say something! Ben, now! Now! NOW!*

That morning, though it took every ounce of strength I could muster, I stood there with my tea and, having nothing to say, remained silent.

I stayed silent for days. If I had something to say, I would say it. I soon discovered, however, that moments of honest, necessary, genuine speech didn't come often.

Noticing the change, a number of fellow students asked me if everything was alright. "Yes," I answered, "I'm doing fine. Thank you." They waited for the next sentence. I wanted to say more. I wanted to detail my waterfall vision and my campaign of silence. *Tell them your story, Ben. Then they'll understand, they'll still like you and you'll be okay.* I knew my demons hid behind this desire to speak. To share my story was to ask for validation. No. I had made a promise to myself. If it meant being ostracized, so be it. I would not speak unless I had something to say.

A few weeks later, we boarded a plane from Tibet to Nepal, from the mystic moon badlands to sweaty, sticky Shangri-La. Back in Kathmandu, drinking chocolate-banana milkshakes and listening to sitar concerts in the funky tourist bookstore, I walked through a world thick with words. Slowly but surely, words shimmied their way back onto my tongue. In cold, razor-edged Tibet, I had received a vision of my own slavery and had demanded freedom. In the comfort of Kathmandu, however, memories of that demonic dance faded. I no longer examined every verbal impulse. I let the words flow.

We don't need to travel to Tibet to witness our addiction to words. We don't need Himalayan waterfalls to introduce us to our demons. I have never returned to Tibet, but I return again and again to silence. I practice silence to see those demons, to prevent them from hiding, to shine a light on what's really going on inside.

As spiritual cross-trainers, we've come to hear God's voice. We can't hear God's voice when we're talking. We can't stop talking if we're addicted to words. We can't cure our addiction to words if our demons run the show. On a search for God, we first search for these demons. We observe the anxious monologues and the compulsive conversations they provoke. We begin by babbling in the darkness. Then we follow a path of silence to the light.

THE PATH OF SILENCE

God wanders the woods. The voice of God meanders through the garden, says the Biblical authors. On a search for God, we go to the garden, to the contemplative corner wherever it may be. No one expects to hear our voice when we stand in the garden. We don't expect to hear theirs. God speaks everywhere, of course, in nature preserves and in Grand Central Station. We don't listen everywhere. The sages, the mystics, the poets—the wisest of the wise move to the quiet places when listening for the voice.

To walk the path of silence, we can enter the woods or sit in a cozy corner of our bedroom. Any quiet place will do. We can sit down or stand up, or, if there's room, walk around. Whatever the body position, we lift our spines, growing tall, with a broad, open chest and a balanced posture, not leaning to one side or the other. Then, we softly gaze at a spot on the floor a few feet in front of us. And we breathe.

On the path of silence, that's all we do. We breathe. Eventually, we may elaborate our practice of silence by spinning a potter's wheel, painting still lifes, or mindfully sipping tea. We may opt to bird watch, to garden or to cloud gaze. If you are a beginner on the path of silence, however, I recommend beginning with the breath alone. This breath will serve as your anchor, your teacher, your shelter in the storm. Then, if your silence takes a different shape one day, if, say, you walk the path of silence with the calligrapher's brush, this breath will be a familiar friend, your old traveling companion, gently, reliably leading you home.

So, in our quiet corner of the globe, sitting, standing, or walking with a gentle gaze upon the ground, we breathe. In through the nose. Out through the nose. We notice the breath, the way it cascades past the throat, the gentle lift of the shoulders and chest in response. We breathe normally. There's no need to hold the breath or exhale until it hurts. We just let the breath do its thing and watch what happens. The breath lives halfway between our conscious and unconscious mind. We spend most of our lives breathing unconsciously, but our breath will react when we pay it attention. At our touch, the breath will settle and purr. Eventually, with time and practice, we will settle and purr, too.

This practice of sitting, standing or walking while noticing the breath has been called by many different names. Some call the practice "mindfulness meditation." Some call it *Shamatha-Vipassana* or Zen. The roots of this practice can be found in the Upanishads, the foundational Hindu scriptures penned at some point in the first millennia BCE. This practice shaped the spiritual life of the Hindu prince Siddhartha Gautama, later known as the Buddha, who, in the fifth century BCE, sat and observed his breath for seven weeks beneath a fig tree. Siddhartha eventually left his arboreal abode to share this practice with his disciples. Centuries later, Buddhists carted the practice south to Sri Lanka, west to the Hellenized Middle East, north to Central Asia, and east into China. In some lands, the meditation practice transformed into a fusion of breath work and visualization. In other lands, the practice focused primarily on the breath. In some communities, practitioners closed their eyes. In other communities, their eyes remained open.

The path of silence I follow was shaped by the Buddhist meditation practices of China and Southeast Asia. The path of meditation I teach has been informed by some of the great sages of contemporary Buddhist thought: His Holiness the Dalai Lama, Thich Nhat Hanh, Trungpa Rinpoche, Pema Chödrön, Zen Master Seung Sahn, and Suzuki Roshi. Still, I maintain no fidelity to any one religion, methodology, sect, or creed. No Buddhist affiliation is required when we walk the path of silence. Our meditation can begin and end with the breath.

I don't want to lie to you. Breathing is boring. And boredom can feel like a small, sad death. Our minds are programmed to fight death at all costs. Our minds detest boredom. So when we practice silence, when we focus on the breath, it will help if we just relax and allow a lot of room for our mind to resist. And resist it will.

Here's what you may notice. You will begin your practice of silence. After a few breaths, or perhaps even before the first exhalation escapes your nostrils, your mind will click and whir. You will think. You will think about the past. You will think about the future. You will talk to yourself, tell stories, replay events, revisit memories, anger yourself with current resentments, and titillate yourself with fantasies. You will worry and want. You will marvel at the wonder of the universe. All of this, even your wonder, even your bliss, will entertain you and leave you breath-less.

Then, like waking from a dream, you will have the thought, "I have been thinking instead of paying attention to my breath." At this point, I recommend saying to yourself, "No big deal." Then begin again, bringing your attention to your breath.

When I first practiced silent meditation, at the age of eighteen, a Zen teacher recommended this practice of observing my thoughts and responding, "No big deal." I didn't listen. I didn't listen because I didn't believe it. I saw myself as a spiritual warrior. Meditation was my battlefield. About to leave for college, I yearned for a solid, sexy identity. I needed a big deal, an activity that would simultaneously engage and impress. In meditation, my mind wandered as much as anyone's, I suppose, but I brought my attention back to my breath with little dreams of future greatness: *Return to your breath, Ben, and return to your true self—one day, you will be a Zen Master.* I made the path of silence a very big deal.

Your response to meditation might go the other way. You may make your wandering mind a big deal, not through self-aggrandizement but through self-denigration. You may try a meditation class and, witnessing the thick current of endless thought, decide: *I'm not good at meditating,* or *I can't sit still,* or *it's just not for me—I prefer to go for a hike.* And you would be right. But you would have also missed the point.

Many who try the path of silence give up too easily. "No big deal" keeps us in the game, on the razor's edge of our experience. We live with whatever bubbles up. We don't glorify. We don't condemn. We care deeply in the way a gardener cares, watching and waiting, patient, determined, accustomed to both famine and feast. We expect boredom and remember that anything worthwhile, including the path to God, takes work and is fun only part of the time.

One evening, while sitting in meditation, following my breath, I suddenly realized in my bones: *All Is Mind.* That night, for whatever reason, I saw how our minds create our entire experience. Every sensation travels through our minds, every sight and sound, every thought. Turn off our minds and we turn off the entirety of what we call existence.

On this one evening, I got it. My cells understood: *All Is Mind.* Suddenly, my field of vision filled with bright, golden light. One second, I sat on my meditation cushion staring at our hardwood floor. The next, my eyes flooded with light. Then it passed. Hardwood floor.

"No big deal" applies to these moments, too. We have occasional revelations and lots of frustrating failures and we say to it all, "No big deal." We understand our place in the universe. We hear the voice of God. *No big deal.* We feel anxious and angry, exhausted and resentful. We want to leave the path of silence and walk a path to the nearest bar. *No big deal.* Whatever happens, we smile a little smile and return to the breath.

Some practitioners like to add a mantra to their meditation, a repeated phrase that hovers upon the breath. The Vietnamese Zen Master Thich Nhat Hanh recommends saying to yourself, "I am breathing in" while inhaling and "I am breathing out" while exhaling. He also recommends counting the breaths. On your first inhalation, you say to yourself, "One." When you exhale, you say again, "One." On your next inhalation, "Two," and so on. When you get to ten, start back again at one. If your mind wanders and you lose count, just say, "No big deal" and start over again at "One." I've had many meditation sessions where I've never gotten past "Two" or "Three." No big deal.

Stillness helps. Even if you're walking in silence, try to keep your arms still by interlacing your fingers and holding your hands in front of your navel. If you're sitting, find a comfortable position that grounds and balances you. Maintain a long, upright spine to help you feel energized. I like to imagine that the crown of my head is holding up the sky. I feel taller, a lot more helpful and a little more hopeful. When I don't achieve my goals, when I can't hold up the sky, no big deal.

The Kabbalists, the Jewish mystics, taught that we live in four worlds at once. We live in the physical world, which they called *Olam Ha-Asiyah.* We live in the emotional world, which they called *Olam Ha-Yetzirah.* We live in the mental world, which they called *Olam Ha-Beriah.* And we live in the world of soul, called *Olam Ha-Atzilut.* When we walk the path of silence, we encounter activity within all four worlds.

During meditation, the physical world, *Olam Ha-Asiyah,* provides us with itches, aches, hunger, lust and exhaustion. Our body doesn't give up, not for a second. Even in stillness we salivate, our bladder fills, we get a random pain in a random place and then, like that, it disappears.

While on the path of silence, we need to remind ourselves that very, very soon we will dive back into *Olam Ha-Asiyah* in full force. We will get up from our meditation cushions and scratch every little itch. We will bounce when we need to bounce. We will doze off. We will eat and drink and make love. So here, just for a little bit of time, rather than react to *Olam Ha-Asiyah*, we keep our body still and we watch. We just watch and learn. No big deal.

I once took this too far. During my sophomore year of college, a few Zen buddies and I took the train to Manhattan to attend a three-day Zen meditation retreat. Over the course of that Zen retreat, seated in meditation for nine hours every day, I made it my goal to sit still. The Zen Center permitted us to stand up behind our meditation cushions if our bodies needed a break, but, at the time, I thought of stillness as a big deal. So when my left knee began to ache, I let it ache. When it throbbed, I breathed through the throb. When it hurt so much I wanted to scream, I mustered my strength and followed my breath. *I am breathing in. Dear God this hurts. I am breathing out. Holy shit I'm dying.* A week later, still limping, I learned through an MRI that I had torn the medial meniscus cartilage in my left knee.

We can practice in stillness without being stupid. If we need to move, we move. Then, having moved, we watch what happens. We follow our breath. No big deal.

In silence, we also encounter activity in *Olam Ha-Yetzirah,* our emotional world. We start sad. Or full of hope. Or something in the physical or mental world triggers an emotional reaction. Suddenly, we rage or desire, delight or despair. Boredom, too, has an emotional texture, an irritating claustrophobia like a one-size too-tight sweater.

In silence, we're emotional explorers. Just as things get hot and intense, just when we would like to break the silence, that's when the real work begins. That's when we dive deep, discovering unknown treasures. A few years ago I attended a one-day silent meditation retreat with twenty other rabbis. During the silent lunch, over a bite of arugula, I began to hear a song that I hadn't heard for a very long time. It cascaded into my consciousness uninvited and I found it hard to continue eating.

The song was one many Chicago natives know by heart. Though raised in Milwaukee, I spent five summers from the ages of nine to thirteen at an all-boys, Jewish summer camp in northern Wisconsin, together with boys from Deerfield, Highland Park, and various other Chicago suburbs. The herd from the Windy City would arrive each summer dressed head to toe in Chicago sports paraphernalia. I came from Chicago's unkempt cousin to the north, but I still joined in when fellow campers would launch into any number of anthems celebrating their beloved White Sox, Cubs, Bulls, and Bears.

During my second year of camp, I heard one particular sports anthem more than others. My cabin counselor, "Lightning" Luke, a college student from Chicago's North Shore suburbs, would sing it to wake us up, to get us riled up at meals and to motivate us on the softball field.

Luke despised me—me and one other equally overweight camper in our cabin by the name of Shelly. With no protection from the guards, Shelly and I suffered plenty. Our bunkmates teased us, bruised us with titty-twisters (if you don't know, you don't want to know), threw our towels mid-shower into the trees, and deftly deposited sand between our folded bed sheets.

One day, Luke called off the dogs and invited Shelly into the circle, albeit a straggler on the outside. Somehow, Shelly had appeased the powers that be. I would have been happy with that fate, but Luke granted me no such amnesty. So the tormenting continued, and at some point, Luke decided he had had enough of watching from the sidelines. He wanted in on the action.

The noise in a summer camp dining hall is not so different from the din at a ballpark. You shout to campers seated right next to you, not noticing that you're shouting because everyone else is shouting. And just like at a ballpark, the crowd occasionally launches into chants and songs. Our camp had lots of fantastic, odd chants, including my favorite:

Hitsu, ratsu, titty-boom-batsu,

I-sitty-I-sy, titty-boom-bah,

Row rah row, siss boom bah!

The ditty was then punctuated by someone's name, or a cabin number, or the name of the camp. Everyone cheered.

I ate a lot at camp. I loved the food—greasy, salty, and abundant. I felt hungry all the time. With the rest of my bunkmates, I entered the dining hall ravenous. Fights erupted over who took the last hot dog. Glasses of fruit punch spilled onto laps and were frantically mopped up with one hand while the other hand continued to ladle spaghetti. I ate and ate, stopping only for chants as they burst spontaneously from various locations in the room.

I don't know why, on this day of days, Lightning Luke decided to take note of my appetite. He may have been hungover. Many counselors spent the beginning of each day hungover from their adventures at the local tavern the night before. Whatever the reason, Luke started cracking jokes at our table about my eating. I can't remember what Luke said to me, but I can remember when, right then and there, he decided to rewrite his favorite sports anthem. As I stared at my lunch plate, nervously smiling, Luke serenaded me again and again, eventually joined by a unison chorus of my bunkmates.

Eat Ben Eat,

Eat Ben Eat,

Shove that food right down your face,

Ben you are a big disgrace.

As I attempted to mindfully eat my arugula, twenty-five years later, I heard this song. I could hear Luke's voice, hoarse and jubilant, directing my cabinmates. Here I sat, the senior rabbi of a synagogue, and at the same time, a camper in Wisconsin's north woods. I was thirty-five years old and ten years old; respected community leader and abused outcast.

During that silent lunch, I suddenly knew: I'd been eating every meal accompanied by this soundtrack. Somewhere in my mind, in shadows usually inaccessible to conscious thought, "Eat Ben Eat" had been playing over and over again. Lightning Luke's clever arrangement lived and breathed, a fungus benefiting from a prime location, just dark enough to prevent discovery but close enough to consciousness to whisper imperceptibly at every meal. Consequently, every bite of food hurt, just a little, enough for me to develop the habit of eating quickly, wolfing my meals to speed through the pain. *My God*, I thought, *I've been doing this for twenty-five years. Twenty-five years.*

As silent explorers of *Olam Ha-Yetzirah*, of our unfathomably complex, emotional world, we may happen upon decades-old scar tissue. Seeing who we are and how we ache, we may be tempted to hold this revelation close to our hearts. *This is me. I'm the boy who was bullied a long time ago. This is the secret hurt that explains who I am.* This identification with our pain is not only unnecessary, it's counterproductive. We don't need to cling to emotional phenomena. When revelation comes, when a song from our past drifts into our present, we only need to see it and then, eventually, if we can, return to the breath. No big deal.

Just by peeking behind *Olam Ha-Yetzirah's* curtain, we have accomplished something wonderful. We've identified an unconscious process that, until now, has controlled our life. This awareness, over time, will allow us to consciously interrupt the emotional patterns that, until now, have seemed inevitable. We will see, for example, that we hurt when we eat and that we rush through our meals as a result. Just by seeing this, we will find ourselves slowing down when we chew.

As silence illuminates *Olam Ha-Asiyah* and *Olam Ha-Yetzirah,* the frenetic dance of our cells and the cryptic complex of our emotions, so it also illuminates *Olam Ha-Beriah,* the world of thought. Meditation presses mute on the world, thrusting us into the jumbled mass of our personal, mental mosh pit. The mind, with its dynamic dance of thoughts, becomes the biggest show in town.

The thoughts that bubble up in silence challenge our self-image and humble us. During one ten-day meditation retreat at a Zen Center near Providence, Rhode Island, I spent a day thinking of nothing but chocolate and sex. Hour after hour, sitting in silence, my mind unwrapped chocolate bars and undressed lovers.

I began that Zen retreat thinking of myself as a brave young warrior exploring exotic lands of the spirit. Poised to climb the mountain, however, I found myself opting for a safe, familiar valley. I chose the entertainment of sensual delights.

Olam Ha-Beriah, the mental world, brims with distractions. It also weighs heavy with judgments. We have a hard time giving the world a break. We want to name it, to figure it out, to decide what's good and bad, and to define right and wrong. In *Olam Ha-Beriah,* we judge each other. And we judge ourselves.

During one Zen retreat, I found myself seated near a tall, balding man, probably in his fifties. I had never met him before this retreat. We hadn't spoken during the retreat's orientation. I knew absolutely nothing about him. Yet, for some inexplicable reason, I detested him. I bristled when he came near. I stole glances at him in meditation, imagining that if we ever had a chance to speak, he'd reveal himself as a grade-A asshole. I started to wonder: do I have some sort of clairvoyance? Has my meditation practice allowed me to sense this man's aura and ascertain his true character?

I asked my Zen Master about this during "Zen interview," a one-on-one meeting between student and teacher. "Do you have any questions?" the Zen Master asked. "Yes," I answered. "I don't know why, but there's a guy in this retreat I can't stand. I've never met him. For all I know, he's a saint. But he just bugs me. What's going on? Why do I feel this way?"

The Zen Master smiled. "This is why we meditate," he began. "We meditate so we can see our minds. We can see that, without even knowing why, we carry prejudice, that we judge each other without any basis for this judgment. What a wonderful thing to see."

Whatever treasures silence reveals, whether physical, emotional, or mental, however beatific or horrific, our job is to look, listen, say "No big deal," and return to the breath. Over and over and over again. Patiently, we wait for the tectonic plates of consciousness to shift. Ninety-nine percent of the time, we won't even detect these shifts. The germination takes place deep in the soil. We just water God's garden patiently and wait with, as my mother says, "high hopes and low expectations." We search for God but we don't depend on God to show up. We depend on ourselves. We show up. Then we wait and see.

Every once in a great while, we may get an earthquake. Four years after beginning the path of silence, on yet another three-day meditation retreat, I lay down on my cot during a rest period and quickly fell asleep. I started dreaming that I was standing on the bank of a river. Turning away from the water, I saw an ex-girlfriend walking toward me, arms outstretched, eyes despairing. She came closer. I retreated, edging backward, toward the water. I looked over her shoulder and saw another ex-girlfriend approaching, and behind her, another. Soon, I stood surrounded by all the women I had dated in high school and college, all the women I had spastically seduced and unceremoniously dropped to prove to myself, again and again, that I was no longer that husky summer-camp outcast. Now, their pained expressions demanded some response on my part. They pushed forward, backing me closer and closer to the water's edge. I could only receive them with the words, "I'm sorry, I'm so sorry," again and again. Then I awoke.

Until that afternoon's catnap, this guilt I'd perpetually shouldered remained the sole property of my unconscious. I continued my harmful campaign of romantic conquest because I honestly did not understand what I was doing, nor the deeper reasons for why I was doing it. During that retreat's afternoon hiatus, for whatever reason, God graced me with revelation.

On the path of silence, we meet ourselves. We discover our ungainly guts. We get to know who we are. No matter what we find, we give ourselves permission to gently smile and say, "No big deal." Then we return to the breath. We stop nowhere, no matter what the revelation, or lack thereof, because getting to know ourselves is not the point. Our demons aren't the point. Our glory or degradation is not the point. We're on a search for God. Our job is to keep searching.

THE SUMMIT OF SOUND

I'm going to tell you a story about hearing God's voice. Our modern age denies prophecy, sequestering would-be prophets to out-of-the-way ministries and mental institutions. Mainstream God-seekers speak in code. We don't claim to hear voices. We "feel" God. We "sense" God is near. But we don't hear God's voice. Not literally. We know where that can lead. To danger, extremism, or worse. I like living in this age, at this time. I feel comfortable knowing that if someone stood on a soapbox and recited a recent missive from God, they'd probably be ignored. After all, I heard the voice of God and yet I remain conflicted and confused. Hearing God's voice thrust me forward on my path, to be sure, but I still live the life of a struggling human being, unsure of my own footing. Hearing God's voice did not make me special. God's voice merely shifted my direction.

I can't, however, pretend that I didn't hear the voice. I can't make that experience go away. I've tried. In fact, when I began writing this book, I took God out of the picture completely. I addressed the spiritual search from a humanistic, health-and-wellness perspective. I wrote lines like, "This is not about God. Love God. Believe in God. Then, with deep devotion, send God out of the room." Reliance upon God, I felt, prevented me from growing up, from taking responsibility for my own life and choices. Rather than coping with life's existential insecurity, I used God as a security blanket. With my thumb in my mouth, eyes wide, I waited for God's will.

What made me change my mind? First, I showed an early draft of this book to my wife, Sara. She read the "send God out of the room" section and frowned. "No," she said, "I don't think this is what you wanted to say." I waited for more. "I just think this section is off the mark," she concluded.

Okay. I've learned to trust Sara on these matters. I tend to get carried away. It takes me time to get in touch with my underlying motivations. For a supposedly wise spiritual leader, I have major blind spots. Sara just knows sometimes. She sees what remains outside my field of vision. So when she read, "send God out of the room," and she said, "No," I'd have been a fool not to pause and reconsider.

The second thing to change my mind? My anger began to subside. I wrote this initial rejection of God in the midst of a crisis of faith. I began my rabbinate a staunch believer in traditional Jewish life and, within a couple years out in the trenches, watched this belief start to unravel. I spent the next two years pretending to believe, and the two years after that leaving my job, moving, and beginning a new life, religiously adrift. Pissed and confused, I sure as hell wanted God out of the room.

But my year of mourning has ended. I'm ready to tell my story.

The voice of God meanders through the garden, say the Biblical authors. What does this voice sound like? What does God say? I feel God every day. I see miracles everywhere. I sense the spark of divinity in my soul. But God's voice? I've only heard it once.

My story begins with the doors of an old Saab slamming shut, one foreboding thud after the next. My younger brother Joel, his college girlfriend Julia, and I stood next to the Saab, pulling our winter coats tightly to our throats. Despite our efforts, Rhode Island's winter air worked its way beneath each layer of fleece and wool. Our teeth chattered as we muttered hurried goodbyes. Joel and Julia looked beyond the field on which we'd parked to a tall pagoda in the distance. Julia, especially, appeared uncomfortable. I didn't blame her. The combination of thin winter air and silence, the absence of any movement, any people, led me to wonder if we'd landed on the moon. But this was not the moon. This was the Rhode Island Zen Center. For the next three months, this would be home.

The Buddha, so the story goes, instructed his followers to spend each winter in prolonged retreat. Beginning each year in early January, the Rhode Island Zen Center offered practitioners three months of silence, ninety days cut off from the outside world, an opportunity to walk in the Buddha's footsteps.

Past participants described this winter retreat as life altering. A few years earlier, before beginning a shorter retreat at the center, I found myself on kitchen duty with a Zen student who had finished her three months the previous winter. The first weeks, she said, tortured her; her mind and body in full-scale revolt. Then something shifted. She sat down one day on her meditation cushion and, out of nowhere, arrived at the deepest stillness she'd ever known. Ever since, she told me, she looked at the world with different eyes.

After college graduation, with no immediate plans and only the vaguest of long-term goals, I decided to go for it. When else would I have ninety days to disappear from the world? Standing now with Joel and Julia at the starting line, however, no glorious promise of self-transformation could buoy me from my dread. What the hell was I doing? I longed to be Joel, to be the brother who didn't need sore knees and silence, who hadn't embarked on a discomforting search for the Creator.

I didn't jump back into the safety of the Saab. Instead, I gave Joel and Julia hugs, told them I'd call them in April, and watched them drive away. Then, nudged forward by blasts of arctic wind, I shouldered my duffle bag and headed inside.

The first day of retreat passed in an adrenaline rush. We few dozen participants bounced through the hallways and sat straight and tall, filled with missionary zeal. By the second day, our spiritual caravan merged onto a long, quiet highway of silence, stillness, and sore knees. Right on schedule, the retreat started to hurt.

I did my job. Though my body hurt and my mind hungered, I followed my breath. Then, the sadness set in. Not a general sadness, but a sharp, pointed ache. *I miss my family. I miss my home.* I had dutifully imparted the instruction to my parents and brother that no correspondence should come my way these three months—no letters or phone calls, except in an emergency. Even while studying abroad in college, I had never gone that long without contact. Sitting on my cushion on day two of the three months, I lamented this radio silence.

What started as a trickle of maudlin nostalgia became, by day three, a torrent of homesickness. *I want to go home.* Here, my Zen training kicked in. *I know what this is,* I told myself. *I've reached the first battleground. This is just natural resistance, to be expected, the cringing of ego under the bright light of the Way.* I returned to my breath. *This is home. Right here. Right now. Breathing in. Breathing out. No big deal.*

Rather than dissipating, my longing for home and family grew ferocious. *I want to go home. What am I doing here? I want to go home.* With every breath, this unwelcome mantra rattled inside my head. My mind flashed a visual image of a calendar, the three months of January, February, and March displayed before me. Each impossibly long month made up of four unbelievably long weeks. Every week composed of endless, cold, silent days. *Oh my God,* I thought. *What have I done?*

By the end of the third day, I had lost my appetite. I couldn't sleep. From the outside, I looked like just another Zen practitioner—gray robed, eyes downturned, serene and silent. Beneath my skin, however, thundered full-scale civil war. *I miss my family. I want to go home. No. This is all you will ever need, right here, right now. Please, I can't. I can't. It's too long. I took on too much. Ben, don't give up. Breathe in. Breathe out. The spiritual warrior must sit in the fire. This is your path. You are home. Oh God, I can't. When will this meditation session be over? How long has it been? I can't. I just can't!*

Itchy, manic, wild, and wretched, I wandered into the woods during the next day's midmorning break. I followed a barely discernible footpath until I could see nothing on all sides but bare, blistered trees. I remember the sky as New England gray, but honestly, it might have been a bright, sunny day. I stopped walking. Silence. I put a hand against the ice-cold trunk of the nearest tree, leaned into that hand and started to speak.

"I'm sorry," I told the trees. "I'm so sorry. I tried. I really tried. But I'm not going to make it. It's time to go home." I let the words settle, hearing my own voice, half expecting the trees to answer. The trees stayed silent. They gave no indication of indictment. At least to them, none of this really mattered. No big deal.

Walking back to the Zen Center, I formulated an exit strategy. Since a number of Zen students couldn't take three months away for the entire retreat, the center allowed students to join the retreat for individual weeks. Every Sunday, some students exited and others entered. Today was Thursday. I would wait until my next one-on-one interview with the Zen Master, which would take place tomorrow. I'd tell him that I needed to leave on Sunday. He'd be disappointed, for sure. Would he dress his disappointment in gentle acceptance or curt disdain? I hoped for the former, but knew that it didn't really matter.

I had stopped eating and sleeping. I had started talking to trees. I was exhibiting all the signs of a nervous breakdown. Time to go.

I entered the meditation hall, a beautiful, long room lined with floor-to-ceiling windows overlooking the woods and the Zen Center's lake. We still had a few minutes left during the break, so I lay down on the floor and, for the sake of my aching knees and back, began a few yoga stretches. With each pose, waves of anxiety and adrenaline coursed up and down my spine. I finished flat on my back, staring up at the white ceiling. Breathing deep.

Then, from out of the depths, I heard myself whisper six Hebrew words:

"Shema Yisrael Adonai Eloheinu Adonai Echad."

Wait a second. Why am I saying this?

"Shema Yisrael Adonai Eloheinu Adonai Echad."

What's going on?

These six Hebrew words passed my lips again and again, each time in a whisper, each time bringing a wave of clarity and calm. Taken from the sixth chapter of the Book of Deuteronomy, the words "Shema Yisrael Adonai Eloheinu Adonai Echad" mean, "Listen Israel—the Lord is our God, the Lord is One." I'd learned these words, known collectively as the "Shema," as a young child in Hebrew school, along with every other Jewish child who'd ever attended synagogue. Even unpracticed, assimilated Jews, who might otherwise stare uncomprehending at their prayer books during services, knew these words. Pilgrims whispered the Shema at Jerusalem's Wailing Wall. Moms, dads, and kids sang them to one another each night. Calligraphed on parchment, the Shema adorned the doorposts of Jewish homes across the globe.

To a twenty-three-year-old Jewish Buddhist, however, none of that mattered. Until this moment, I had grouped the Shema together with other spiritually irrelevant cultural icons. To me, the Shema belonged with matzo balls and Woody Allen movies. Even in the midst of a breakdown, whispering the Shema didn't make sense. Neither did the undeniable fact that, with each repetition, my edgy, exhausted panic began to subside.

When I stood up for the next meditation session, I felt deeply relaxed. I buzzed with a primal, visceral clarity. I sat down on my cushion. The monk leading our meditation sessions took up a long, wooden clapper and slapped it against his palm three times, letting us know the next session had begun.

Immediately, my knees began to ache. I stood up behind my cushion, hands together in prayer, waiting for the pain to subside. While in retreat, we students had received the instruction to keep our eyes downcast. We were told that looking into each other's eyes or out the window at the pretty view was just our mind seeking entertainment, looking for a way out. In my current state, however, that directive seemed ridiculous. I raised my eyes from the floor to the floor-to-ceiling windows in front of me. The day's beauty, the brilliant shimmer of frozen pond, tangled trees, and hills beyond, flooded my eyes.

I softened my focus, taking in the peripheral view of fellow retreat participants on either side. Their serene beauty blended with the natural vista beyond. I saw us as the trees saw us—odd, lovely creatures, sitting together in matching robes, silently striving to transform. How wonderful! And how meaningless, too. We sat here because *we wanted to sit here*. We sat here because we imagined there was a self to transform. But the trees knew better. No spiritual wilderness to traverse. No enlightenment to achieve. We sat here because we liked it. That was it.

And me, I didn't like it anymore. *I. Was. Done.*

This would be my final meditation session at the retreat. I just knew. During the next break, I would quietly pack my bag and slip away. Upon this new exit strategy's formulation, however, I felt a huge surge of energy course though my body. My eyes opened wide.

SPEAK

The word exploded. Every cell of my body had suddenly tuned to the same frequency, broadcasting this message. The word shook my toes. The word whispered from the hairs on my head. My entire body pulsed.

SPEAK

Again, the word tore through me. *Oh my God,* I thought. *Is this? Is this God?* I knew the answer. Knew it in my bones.

SPEAK

THANK THEM FOR THEIR LOVE

No, I thought, *I don't want to. I know who You are. But I don't want to. Just let me leave quietly. Just let me go.*

Silence. No answer.

I inhaled. I exhaled. I opened my mouth and said in a loud, clear voice, "Thank you for your love." Then I turned and walked toward the exit.

"Bullshit."

This word slammed into me from behind. I recognized its origin. The voice, clear, decisive, with only the faintest trace of emotion, belonged to the Zen Master.

I didn't stick around to get clarification. I hurried down the steps to the residence rooms. I entered my room and began packing my things.

Suddenly, I heard footsteps pounding on the floor above me, then down the stairs. With a flurry of long gray robes, the Zen Master charged into my room, eyes wide with rage.

He came within a few inches of me and pointed his finger at the tip of my nose. "Thank you for your love?!" he spat in a furious whisper. "Thank you for your love?! That's bullshit and you know it! You, with your parents, your money, your good situation. There are people here who are practicing and trying their hardest—there's a woman here who is mentally ill! But they come and do their best. And here you show up and ruin their practice!"

"Hold on," I stammered. He didn't understand. He didn't know what had happened. He didn't know about the voice.

"No," he growled, stepping even closer. "You listen to me. One day you're going to get cancer. Maybe not today, maybe not tomorrow, but it will happen. And then what will you do? You won't be able to run away. You won't have an escape. What will you do?"

He didn't wait for my reply. He simply stepped back, spun around and walked away. Then, just before he turned out of sight, he looked back one last time.

"Get a life."

And he was gone. I continued to gather up my things, more slowly this time. I felt tired and dizzy. Then, an urgent thought popped into my head: *Nobody is expecting to hear from me for three months.* Everything, the breakdown, the revelation, the goodbye, the chastisement, faded into the background, replaced by one clear directive: *I have to get out of here. Now. Right now!*

I threw my things in my bag, zipped it up and bounded up the stairs. The hallway and lobby area remained empty, everyone still in meditation. I exited the center, jogged down the hill, past the lake, up the driveway and past the pagoda. And suddenly, like leaving a movie theater and entering the outside world, I passed through the Zen Center's gate onto an empty, quiet, farm-lined road. No big deal.

Eventually, I made it to a larger road. I saw a flower shop across the street. Maybe they'd have a phone. When I entered, the woman behind the counter greeted me warmly. If I had any questions, she said, feel free to ask. I meandered between brightly colored bouquets, trying to figure out my next move. I needed to find a place to sit for a while and regroup. Maybe get some food, too.

"Excuse me," I said to the woman, approaching the counter. "I realize this is a strange question. But I'm a little lost and could really use a lift. I think there's a diner just a few miles down the road. Would there be any way you might be willing to give me a ride? I promise, I'm just a regular guy in a tight spot. If you could help, that would be really great."

I waited. The woman looked at me for a moment, sizing up the situation.

"Okay," she said, smiling. "No problem. Just give me a minute to close up."

Five minutes later, having thanked the flower lady profusely, I sat at a small booth amid the diner's late-morning patrons, a glass of water and a glass of orange juice placed before me. When I reached for the water, I noticed my hand shaking. Both hands—I couldn't make them stop. I took a few deep breaths, then got up to use the pay phone.

First, I called an old friend, another Ben, a student at Brown University in nearby Providence. Thankfully, he picked up the phone.

"Listen, Ben, I'll explain later, but I really need a ride. I'm stuck out by the Zen Center. It's not that far from Providence. Is there any way you could come pick me up?"

Ben didn't own a car, but he told me he'd figure out something.

"Just stay there," he said. "I'll come get you."

I put another quarter into the pay phone and dialed home. My father worked from home most mornings, so it didn't surprise me to hear his voice on the other end of the line.

"Dad," I said.

"Ben?" He instantly sounded concerned. "Are you okay?"

I didn't give a lot of details. I told him I left the retreat. I told him it wasn't my path anymore. I told him I didn't want to be out of touch from everyone for three months. I told him I'd be fine, that Ben was on his way to pick me up and that I'd be home soon.

Then I asked him, not even sure why I was asking, my voice choking up, my eyes filling with tears, "Dad, are you angry with me?"

My father's voice turned consoling, "No, honey, of course not. Not in the least. Do you remember what you told me a couple weeks ago? I asked you why you wanted to go on this retreat. You told me that you wanted to 'wake up.' Well, the way I see it, you woke up."

I promised to call my dad from Ben's apartment in Providence. After we hung up, I walked back to my booth. As I nursed my orange juice and water, the reality of the past few hours began to sink in. This journey, begun five years earlier when I entered a Unitarian Church in downtown Milwaukee for my first Zen meditation session, had abruptly ended. My long-held secret desire, shared with no one, not even my parents and closest friends, that I might one day become a Zen monk myself, that I might follow in the footsteps of my Zen Master, blissful and bald, had vanished.

Despite my father's reassurance, I felt alone in a diner in Wherever, Rhode Island, like an absolute failure. I'd stepped off my path. God had spoken to me, yes. But so had my teacher. *Get a life.* He was right. I had no life. I had no plans. I was just a guy with a glass of juice waiting for a ride with nowhere to go.

The folks in the booth across the aisle started getting up, chatting and laughing happily as they put on their coats. I noticed one of them in particular rising from his seat. A bearded man probably in his forties, he wore long brown robes with a giant silver cross hanging from his neck.

I looked into his eyes. He looked into mine. Without thinking, I opened my mouth. "Excuse me. Do you mind if I ask you a question?"

The others at his table had already made their way to the diner entrance. The man in robes sat back down, eyes locked with mine.

"Please," he said.

I looked down, then back up to him. "Does God discriminate? Does God love us, all of us?"

Why was I asking this?

The stranger didn't hesitate. "God doesn't discriminate. God loves us all."

I nodded. "Thank you," I said. Then I turned back to my orange juice.

The man in robes stood up, but didn't move away.

"Just give me a minute," he said. He walked over to the others waiting for him at the entrance. He said something I couldn't hear. The others left quietly. He walked back and sat down across from me in my booth.

"My name is Father Kadri," he said. "Are you alright? What's going on?"

I didn't mention God's voice. I told him about the retreat, about having a nervous breakdown and about the Zen Master's response. When I finished, I waited for the inevitable invitation to begin a friendship with Jesus. But Father Kadri didn't mention Jesus.

"You don't know me, but I want to give you some advice," he said. "You seem lost. Go home. Go spend some time with your family. You've been in the clouds. You're shaken up. Go home and find the ground beneath your feet."

I nodded. I didn't know what else to say. Father Kadri stayed with me, making small talk, until my friend Ben walked through the door. Ben didn't own a car, so he had gone to Brown University's Catholic chaplain to ask for a ride. Thus, the Jewish ex-Buddhist left the company of one priest and hitched a ride with another.

After a few days crashing at Ben's apartment, I followed Father Kadri's advice and boarded a plane for Milwaukee. For the next six months, I lived with my parents, working odd jobs and strolling Milwaukee's still, gray tundra. I visited and revisited the memory of the retreat, of the breakdown, of God's voice. I analyzed every detail, studying the memories like scripture, searching for any guidance I might use to navigate this early-twenty-something aimless abyss.

Now, nearly fifteen years later, I still haven't deciphered the meaning of my divine encounter. I don't know what happened. I don't know how it happened. Most importantly, I don't know *why* it happened. I suspect that God's voice works upon us the way love works upon us. God's voice bypasses our brains and works directly through our cells. It vibrates our very atoms. If we're still and silent, listening closely, wandering deep into the garden, we might hear something. With the word, God will move us where we need to go.

PART II:

STRETCH

THE VALLEY OF THE STIFF NECK

Over three thousand years ago, a tribe of slaves clawed its way from the killing fields of Egypt. Assailed by nomads and crippled by thirst, they wandered the wilderness of Sinai, reaching the foot of the holy mountain only to have their prophet and protector disappear beyond its peak. Moses was with a God they could not see, leaving them at base camp to wait and worry. They panicked. They gathered together their valuables, melted them down and forged a new protector, a god of gold.

It was here, at the moment of my ancestors' greatest misstep, the golden calf barely cooled in their hands, that God condemned the Children of Israel with the words: *This is a stiff-necked people* (Ex. 32:9). The golden calf demonstrated the Children of Israel's obstinacy and inflexibility. Like a yoked ox refusing to turn its head at the pull of the reins, the Jewish people stiffened their necks and refused to turn from their well-trod path of idolatry. God employed the anatomical image— *stiff neck*—to describe this defect of character.

What if the metaphoric condemnation—*This is a stiff-necked people*—also served as a literal diagnosis? Looking down upon the Children of Israel gathered around their molten abomination, what if God noticed how these obstinate, inflexible and impenetrable individuals all suffered from a common physical affliction? What if the Children of Israel actually had stiff necks?

Traumatized by generations of slavery and genocide, anxious regarding the uncertainty of newfound freedom, my ancestors had good reason to tense up. They existed in a permanent state of fight-or-flight, necks and shoulders tender and tight. Such tight necks could constrict important lines of communication between mind and body, between head and heart. A people so literally disembodied might rationalize idolatry without giving their bodies a chance to veto. Gazing upon the resulting insanity, and perceiving the physical embodiment of this spiritual error, God responded accordingly: *This is a stiff-necked people.*

I am the descendent of this confused congregation. I have a stiff neck. Both a metaphorical stiff neck and a literal, physical, flesh-and-blood ache. My neck hurts. Not every minute. Not even every day. But much of the time. I have a photo someone took of me at age fifteen. In the photo, I am offstage during a theater rehearsal reading a book. My arm is tucked behind my head and, not taking my eyes from the book, I am massaging my neck. Here we are, over twenty years later, and, whether reading, watching television, or sitting at the computer, my hand continues its commute to neck, shoulder and jaw.

I discovered the depth of my discomfort, and the ecstasy of its release, as a college student living and studying in India. Prior to dancing with demons in Tibet, I spent two months in Dharamsala, a tiny North Indian town, sandwiched on the south by rolling foothills and on the north by ferocious, snowcapped peaks. Dharamsala nurtured a fascinating mix of Indian natives, Tibetan transplants, and Western seekers, all winding past one another on the town's narrow, steep, unpaved roads.

As a center for Tibetan culture in exile, Dharamsala hid incredible treasures in its ramshackle apartment buildings and dilapidated huts. Some of Tibet's greatest scholars and most revered sages lived and taught out of their living rooms. Reincarnated lamas passed on the street before heading down tiny dirt paths to their humble abodes. The town felt otherworldly, magical—every day a discovery. As a budding student of religion, I wandered through Shangri-La.

I also wandered in pain. My shoulders hurt. My neck ached. Looking back, I see how the combination of altered diet, lack of exercise and traveler's stress exacerbated my symptoms. At the time, however, I didn't care why I hurt—I just wanted it to stop.

I had heard in my travels that, while one might choose a Western clinic for broken bones or amoebic dysentery, traditional Tibetan medicine worked wonders for chronic conditions. Neck and shoulder pain? Ibuprofen might calm the symptoms. Tibetan medicine could provide the cure.

After my initial weeks in Dharamsala, I met a Tibetan translator named Tenzin, a sweet, soft-spoken man in his late twenties or early thirties, face heavily pockmarked, always dressed in a button-down, slacks, and a threadbare, wool sweater. Tenzin began helping me with a research project on Tibetan dream theory. One day as we walked home from a field interview, I asked Tenzin if he knew of a good Tibetan doctor to help me with my shoulder and neck pain. Tenzin asked around, and within a few days we found ourselves seated in the living room of an elderly Tibetan monk, complete with smoothly shaven head and flowing maroon robes. Tenzin explained that, in addition to his monastic calling, this monk happened to be a revered practitioner of Tibetan medicine.

The doctor, speaking only Tibetan, asked about my background and reason for visiting Dharamsala. Then he began his examination.

First, I gave him the disposable water bottle of urine I had collected earlier that day, per the doctor's instructions. He held it up to the window's sunlight for a few moments, examining its hue. He then placed his fingers upon my wrist, divining the intricacies of my pulse.

These preliminaries concluded, the doctor asked me to remove my shirt and lie facedown on his sofa. Without a word of explanation, he began vacuum-sealing teacup-sized glass vials to different areas of my back and shoulders. When he ran out of vials, the doctor picked up actual teacups from his coffee table. He then lit small pieces of paper, threw them in the cups and slapped the cups onto my back. The sudden lack of oxygen extinguished the flames and created an equally effective vacuum seal.

A virtual porcupine, back striated with glass, I sat there thinking: *This is so cool!* While most of my college buddies had opted to remain stateside for their junior years, or had ventured only as far as London or Paris, here I was, on the other side of the planet, receiving therapy for neck pain from a Tibetan monk. All this passed through my mind, followed by a very different thought: *Whoa, I don't feel so good.*

I awoke with no idea where I was. Opening my eyes, I looked up into the smiling face of an old Tibetan man. "Hello," he said, eyes twinkling, cradling my head in his lap. A few seconds more and it all came back to me. This smiling face belonged to the doctor, who was now slowly helping me to a sitting position. I looked around the room, getting my bearings. Tenzin sat a few feet away, looking concerned. I offered him a smile, hoping to reassure him.

For a while, I just sat there, feeling like I had emerged from the longest sleep of my life. My body had every intention of melting onto the floor. The doctor, unfazed, began filling small plastic baggies with marble-sized pills, all different shades of brown and maroon. He scribbled notes and numbers onto a small piece of paper; apparently, a prescription for which pills to take when. The doctor handed me the pills and the instructions. Then he smiled and ushered us to the door.

As we stood in the doorway, I turned to Tenzin and asked him to translate one more question. In addition to taking the pills and changing my diet, I asked, should I make any other changes in my lifestyle or behavior? Tenzin translated. The doctor listened, then smiled. Should I make any changes in my behavior? "Yes," he answered, switching to English. "Relax."

We left the doctor's home, thanking him with hands pressed together in prayer. Tenzin asked if I was okay. I was more than okay. I felt incredible. My body felt simultaneously grounded to the earth and light as air. My neck pain and shoulder tension—completely gone.

I thanked Tenzin and continued on alone, meandering up one of Dharamsala's narrow streets. Tibetans and Indians wove past me and each other, finishing their late-afternoon errands. I had grown used to the wild bazaar that is an Indian street. Now, however, the world around me shimmered. Colors exploded. Sounds cascaded bright and brilliant. My senses took in the surroundings without anxiety or agenda. I smiled to those I passed, feeling gratitude for the reassuring warmth of their company. I looked up—high altitude mountain sky delighted in blues and whites. *Relax.* Of course. How sweet. How very right. *Relax.*

By the next morning, my anxiety had returned. The sky, the streets, the passersby—yesterday's miracles now reverted to today's same old. My body, loose and relaxed a day ago, started stockpiling tension minute by minute. No, I had not received a miracle cure. I had been granted a temporary release. A taste of freedom.

Not all had been lost. I still had the doctor's prescription. *Relax.* If I wanted to see the world through God's eyes, if I hoped to wake up to the miraculous quality of my everyday life, if I wanted a life without chronic tension in my neck and shoulders, I needed to relax. But how? As one Zen teacher had taught me, "We live on the planet of fear." Sure, we humans have exited the food chain. We hold the keys to the kingdom. Yet, we know in our bones what waits for us. Old age. Sickness. Death. Our existential awareness, our knowledge of mortality, prevents us from relaxing. How can we possibly relax when allowed this peek behind the curtain?

Most of us relax by distracting ourselves. We climb down from our existential lookout posts and return to ground level, focusing here and now. If mortality comes knocking at our door, if the sickness or death of someone we know causes our brow to furrow and our blood pressure to rise, we distract ourselves until the knocking stops. Mortality, meanwhile, hasn't gone away. It's simply crept to the back porch, slipping in through the doggy door and building a cozy nest in the basement. Out of sight, out of mind, mortality bangs the pipes while we sleep. It giggles from beneath the floorboards as we charge through our day. Death tickles our nerves—we grow edgy and anxious, not sure why. We grab for a cigarette, a drink, a remote control, a bite to eat or a body to caress. We check Facebook. We work out. We vie for that promotion. We grow addicted to whatever provides relief. All the while, our roommate grows comfortable and cavalier.

When the doctor cupped my back, he flushed anxiety from my basement. He reminded me what it might feel like to live without mortality gnawing at my nerves. I walked home lighter, like a parent of young children who, after scores of toddler-laden, folding-stroller plane trips, suddenly boards a flight by himself and can't believe the miracle before him. All that time. All that space. Dharamsala's streets shimmered with a new coat of paint because my conscious mind had the time and space to enjoy and explore. Everything had changed because I had changed. For a few precious hours, I had been released from the planet of fear, free to play in the fields of the Lord.

The doctor had provided me a taste of liberation. He had not articulated a strategy for accomplishing this same feat on my own. How could I fulfill the doctor's prescription without daily doses of cupping and fainting? How would I relax when, in the rush of daily life, I didn't even know I was afraid?

Over and over, I replayed the treatment in my mind. When the doctor cupped my back, the resulting relaxation in my body triggered relaxation in my mind. Without any overt discussion of my fears, without hours on the couch in psychoanalysis, physical relaxation had produced psychological relaxation. Could this chain reaction operate in reverse? If bodily sensation rippled through the mind, wouldn't thoughts, even unconscious thoughts, ripple through the body? Could an anxious mind, burdened by subtle, subconscious fears, trigger a detectable, flesh-and-bone tension? Might a God-seeker, burdened with fear yet consciously unaware of this spiritual stumbling block, look to his stiff neck as a reliable, early warning system, a canary in the coal mine of consciousness?

I had always viewed my stiff neck as a nuisance. What if, in fact, nestled reliably upon my shoulders dwelled my most dependable ally? If I began to lose my way, this highly sensitive instrument for measuring stress would respond. First, a barely perceptible discomfort. Then, a dead-tissue numbness. Finally, a painful stiffening, accompanied by fused jaw and rising shoulders. All in direct relation to stress.

If I listened to my neck in these moments, if I stepped back on the path of relaxation by stopping my desperate chase, taking a breath and offering a little prayer to God for the miracle of my life, perhaps the process would reverse. My shoulders would edge back from my ears. My jaw would release. My neck would loosen. My hand would return from its massage duties to more regularly scheduled activities.

Each of us has a stiff neck, a part of our body that, lacking the convenience of an on-off switch, provides minute-by-minute reports on our emotional and spiritual well-being. Perhaps our neck and shoulders ache. Or we get migraines. Maybe our lower backs give out. Or we compulsively eat. Perhaps we need pills to sleep. Or we just can't climb from the couch. Whatever the early warning system, when fear courses down our spines, when stress tangles our nerves, our bodies respond. Whether we like it or not, our bodies are truth tellers, pointing out our wayward wandering, acknowledging the fear we've furtively tried to sweep under the rug.

When our bodies rumble, we have two choices. We can take the hint, bypassing another scotch and instead slowing down, taking a few deep breaths, looking around and making time and space for God's world to shimmer once more. Or, when the body speaks, we can choose not to listen. You might think, after floating blissfully down a Dharamsala street, that I would start listening to my stiff neck. I did not. Human beings have the capacity to forget even the most astounding of revelations. After Dharamsala, very little changed for me, at least on the inside. I returned home, completed my undergraduate studies and began my compulsory years of early-twenty-something drifting. Eventually, I moved to Israel, met my wife Sara, fell in love, and the two of us rented an apartment in Jerusalem, blocks from the rabbinical school where I would begin my graduate work.

That's when my neck revolted. It could be ignored for only so long. In the midst of Israel's second intifada, the stress choking all of Jerusalem, my neck enlisted the whole of my nervous system to stage its own rebellion. I'd be sitting in class, struggling to conjugate Hebrew verbs, and suddenly, I couldn't breathe. My heart pounded in my ears, growing more rapid by the minute. I couldn't hear what the professor was saying. In my mind, she sounded like a teacher in a *Peanuts* TV special: *"Wah WAH, wah WAH, wah WAH . . ."*

I stumbled outside, trying to make it look like I was headed for the bathroom, and collapsed in one of the campus's outdoor alcoves, a small, grassy nook surrounded by walls of Jerusalem stone. There I lay, grass tickling the backs of my arms, the trickling of a nearby fountain in my ears, gazing through branches and leaves to the blue sky beyond.

As that year in Jerusalem rolled on, as buses exploded and all of Israel hunkered down for the next eternity of turmoil, these panic attacks grew more frequent. Each one left me not only incapacitated in the moment, but exhausted for hours afterward. I grew irritable, challenging Sara's patience and straining our relationship. Even if I had remembered the lessons of Dharamsala, I couldn't have applied them to my current circumstances. I had moved beyond a stiff neck. I was falling apart.

For those of us who imagine ourselves indestructible, who might nurse a secret wish in our hearts that we'll be elected the next messiah, popping an antidepressant takes courage. One of the bravest things I've ever done was to visit a kindly psychiatrist in Jerusalem who prescribed 150 milligrams a day of an antidepressant called Effexor. Immediately, my panic attacks subsided. A bus blowing up down the block no longer landed me on my back. I stayed on my feet and stayed in the game.

Even when returning from Israel to the states, getting married, finishing school, beginning a career, and celebrating the births of our two children, I continued my daily dose of Effexor. I never imagined with that first pill that I had begun a medicinal regimen that would last a decade and beyond. I considered tossing my pills plenty of times. Then I'd remember that walls-closing-in suffocation, that flat-on-the-floor collapse. Now a rabbi, a husband, and a father, I couldn't afford those daily defeats.

So I swallowed my little pink pills and accepted détente. We moved to Boston, where I took a position as senior rabbi of a small suburban synagogue. Sara worked as the admissions director for a small college down the road. We bought a house. We planted a garden. We took the T to Fenway Park and Boston Common. We started to settle.

Smack in the middle of these years, we Shalvas four piled into our minivan one weekend and drove to the home of Sara's cousin Dave. Dave, his wife, Allie, and their two young sons lived in a large, high-ceilinged home just outside West Hartford. They also occupied a political and social netherworld. Politically conservative gun-owning back-to-the-landers, they simultaneously opposed Western medicine and refused to eat anything that wasn't carefully shepherded from farm to fridge. A diplomatic miracle had allowed books by Ann Coulter and Michael Pollan to cuddle on their bookshelves.

As part of their health-without-hospitals agenda, Dave and Allie attended Bikram Yoga classes at a studio just minutes from their home. On this particular visit, as our kids played together in the snow, Allie invited us to join her for a yoga class while Dave watched the kids. Why not? I had practiced yoga on and off since college; it had always been a prelude to other activities, a few yoga postures before a workout or a meditation session. Though I'd hardly call the yoga I'd done profound or transformative, I'd enjoyed the stretch. Yoga was nice. So, sure, we're on vacation, the kids are enjoying themselves, let's do some yoga. Nice.

Sara had gone to a class with Allie on a previous visit. As we drove to the studio, she walked me through the details. Every Bikram Yoga class, from beginning to end, was exactly the same. The same postures, the same words from the teacher, the same ninety-minute duration, and, yes, the same 105-degree heat. It was totally fine, Sara explained, to lie down any time you felt dizzy or overwhelmed. "Just don't leave the room," Allie added. "The teachers hate that." Okay, I thought, this will be a different kind of nice. Not a flowy-linen, incense-infused, shanti-shanti kind of nice, but a kick-ass, sweaty, can't-wait-for-this-fucking-thing-to-be-over kind of nice.

That morning, the teacher led us through a wonderful class. She challenged without chastising. She inspired without inflating egos. Where the yoga I'd known to this point had sandwiched gentle stretching with positive affirmations, this class combined exacting reverence for technique with a no-frills, anti-new-age agenda. Yoga, according to Bikram, needn't feel good. Push yourself! Break down and break through. Yoga by Bikram introduced you to your edge. There, at your edge, things happened. Things like courage, like strength, like healing.

I can't say I found courage, strength, or healing that first class. I stayed in the room. I approximated the majority of the postures. I didn't spew my breakfast. And I even felt pretty good afterward. By the afternoon, though, I merged back into the rush hour of parenthood and, save for a mild headache that hovered by my temples, forgot all about the class.

The following morning, I snuck away and wandered down Dave and Allie's driveway for a cigarette. At that point, I smoked one or two cigarettes a week; a habit I normally combined with visits to my therapist, smoking in her parking lot before or after a session. I smoked to wave the white flag. I smoked to remind myself that, while I might hunger for perfection in all that I did and all that I was, a small part of me wanted to light up and not give a fuck. Each time therapy brought me face to face with this inner child of apathy and anger, each time I entertained the notion that loving this child would do me a lot more good than fixing him, I punctuated this revelation with a smoke. I was broken, and no number of degrees, accolades or accomplishments would change that fact. So be it. Inhale. Hot smoke pours into lungs. Body relaxes. Exhale. So be it.

Fingers stinging on that cold Connecticut morning, I lit my cigarette and offered a brief prayer of thanks for these quiet, family-free five minutes. Then, to my surprise, I realized that, for the first time since beginning this little ritual of relatively benign smoke breaks, I didn't want the cigarette that burned slowly between my fingers. I took another drag, held it, looked at the trees, exhaled. Nope. It just didn't feel good to me. I felt like I was choking myself. I put the cigarette out in the snow. *Hmmm. Interesting.*

The following day, I was soaring. Some kind of endorphin echo-effect had kicked in. I couldn't believe how good I felt. And I couldn't wait to get back to a Bikram studio. If a first class had me chucking my American Spirits and floating a few inches off the ground, what might a week of classes do? Or a month?

I hit the web, located a Bikram studio fifteen minutes from our home and showed up thirty minutes early for the following morning's 9:15 class. The studio, delightfully understated, cozy in an age of yoga-gone-corporate, sat sandwiched between a tanning salon and a party store in an otherwise forgettable suburban strip mall. The teacher, an equally understated woman with the body of a sprite and a quiet, calming demeanor, welcomed me, gave me the tour and then showed me to the yoga room. For the second time in three days, I sweated and stretched. And for the second time in three days, I felt fantastic.

During the next few months, that strip mall became my Jerusalem, the yoga studio my Temple Mount. I drove to my suburban shrine three times a week. Despite drowning myself in coconut water and electrolyte supplements, I nursed a mild headache that began with my morning yoga class and ended when I fell asleep at night. I didn't care. The next month, I upped it to four times a week. Then five.

Sara, equally bedazzled by her newfound Bikram-honed body and mind, attended classes three to four times a week, sometimes leaving the house at six to catch an early morning sweat before work. Though we rarely attended class together, one of us working or parenting while the other one stretched, we met each evening to share tales of our yoga adventures. Who had taught that day? How had each posture felt? Any breakthroughs? Wasn't this incredible? We didn't know it at first, but we had fallen in love.

At the beginning of every class, our teachers would ask us to stand on our mats, feet together, arms by our sides, and just look at ourselves in the floor-to-ceiling mirrors. "This is your territory," they would say. "The goal is you. Listen and get to know yourself." Then we began to stretch. And listen. I listened to my thoughts. I listened to my emotions. I listened to my body. Day after day, month after month, year after year, I listened.

My body began to tell its secrets. Yoga yanked on every region of the body, introducing me to previously unknown muscles, tendons, ligaments and organs. My hips stopped being my "hips." They differentiated into my tight psoas, my tender TFL, and in the back, the devil itself—my curmudgeon of a piriformis. As I discovered this inner landscape, I began to detect minute shifts in the terrain, both on and off the mat. My body no longer had to shout to get my attention. Now, when the body whispered, I listened.

And that is how, twelve years after waking up in that Tibetan doctor's arms with a loose neck and an open heart, I started listening to my disagreeable, cranky, incredulous, wise and wonderful stiff neck. I listened, for example, on those mornings when, Sara having already left for work, I was up with our two children, ages eight and five, getting them ready for school. I'd start the morning blearily mixing oatmeal and arranging backpacks, eyes darting from clock to kids to clock again. We had to be out the door by 7:30 a.m. If not, they'd be late to school, their future delinquency resting squarely on my shoulders.

My kids, on the other hand, could care less about the clock. They wanted to commandeer my cell phone. They wanted to fight. They wanted to build a tower of Legos. As our interests collided, my stress increased. I frantically ran up and down stairs to fetch socks and toothbrushes. I took shallow breaths if I breathed at all. *It's 7:21! Will we make it?*

On such a perfectly average morning, living the suburban dream, attacking parental responsibilities with a more or less winning record, my neck had begun to throb. But now, as a practitioner of yoga, trained to detect and respond to minute changes beneath the skin, I decided to listen. I stopped, took some deep breaths and looked around. There sat my two children, fighting over who could use the purple crayon. My hands cradled a cup of coffee, sweet and warm. I felt my feet on the floor and rolled my weight over the whole of each foot, relishing this secret little dance. African-style electric guitar riffs whined from my favorite online radio station. It was cold or hot, rainy or sunny, and we were okay.

As I noticed all this and, at least for the moment, let go of the clock, my neck pain subsided. As I indulged in the morning's sensations, the muscles in my neck, shoulders and jaw responded with release. A warmth flooded my jaw, a comforting heaviness settled in my shoulders and I even felt some goose bumps down my arms. I'd given in to my neck's demands and now received its tribute and gratitude.

On the path of stretching, our body transforms from dutiful servant to treasured friend. We listen to this friend. We honor our flesh. We value bodily missives, even the ones we find inconvenient. Just as our friends don't always make sense, don't always do what we want, and don't always return our calls, and just as we dilute disappointment with love and forgiveness, we do the same now with our ungainly bag of bones. Our stiff necks implore us, again and again: *Relax*. We can buy a ticket to India and get cupped in the Himalayan hills or we can stop what we're doing, right here, right now, and listen. *Relax*. Maybe we don't want to relax. If we relax, the kids might be late to school. *Relax*. If the kids are late to school, we'll be that parent who just can't get their shit together. *Relax*. *Relax*. *Relax*.

On the planet of fear, we've determined just the right speed to outrun our demons. Gritting our teeth, clutching our gods of gold, we busy ourselves at the mountain's base. As seekers, however, we're called to climb. The climb will require a level of calm and clarity extending from skin to nerves to bone. Indeed, God doesn't just wait for us on the mountain's peak. God hides behind the macramé of our nerves. God waits for us in the nuclei of our cells. So we listen to our stomachache, our pounding temples, our rising shoulders, our stiff necks. We take a leap of faith and relax.

THE PATH OF STRETCHING

On the path of stretching, we are scientists and poets.

The ancient yogis, who developed yoga in India between 1500–500 BCE, operated with a scientific mind and a poetic heart. As scientists, they sought to understand the mysteries of the universe. B.K.S. Iyengar, the yogic scholar and sage, explains, "Indian yogis were trying to see some pattern in the seemingly chaotic fluctuations of Nature. The infinite variety of natural phenomena gives an appearance of chaos, but, they asked, is it possible that the laws that govern the unending turbulence of nature are orderly and comprehensible? And if we can grasp how they work, would it not be possible for us to emerge from chaos into order?" Through contemplative practices, which gave birth, over the next thousand years, to a path of stretching called Hatha Yoga and a variety of poses called *asanas,* these yogis hoped to glimpse the blueprints of creation, creation beyond their bodies and creation beneath their skin.

As we practice Hatha Yoga, as we stretch toward God in each asana, we stretch as scientists. We diagram our inner terrain and the connection between cells and soul. We treat every observation with attention and reverence. If, after tossing and turning all night, we explode, brilliant on the mat, the scientist in us takes note. *Ah—that's interesting!* When we notice that our body always wants to throw its weight into the right leg more than the left, we record this valuable data.

As scientists, we must pay attention not only to our bodily sensations, but also to our emotions and our thoughts before, during, and after we stretch. How do we feel about what's happening to us at this moment? What commentaries run through our heads? For years, in yoga practice, I found myself eager and optimistic during the standing asanas and tired and resistant during the floor asanas. Then, out of the blue, it switched. I found myself impatient to get through the standing asanas so I could get to the floor. As an aspiring scientist, researching the fluctuations of my head and heart, I took note. I didn't judge. I didn't applaud or condemn. I just took note.

We don't necessarily have to understand what we discover. That's where the scientific metaphor breaks down. We're not actually scientists, pressured for plausible hypotheses. Scientists of stretching do exist. These bona fide experts explain the mechanisms by which muscles tense and release. They write textbooks diagramming the pathways of weight traveling through our bones. This knowledge can help our yoga practice. But it's a sidebar for the seeker.

As spiritual cross-trainers, we temper the scientific mind with a poetic heart. Like a scientist, the seeker stretches to observe and understand, to visit every cell and hear its secrets. But like a poet, the seeker tunnels through the body to behold its complexity with awe and wonder.

Stretching thwarts our every expectation. We think we've learned something. We think we finally understand how the body ticks. We think we know when to expect a storm of emotions and how to trigger clarity of mind. But the yoga mat surprises us. We don't get it. We've guessed wrong. When we turn our bodies upside down and twist ourselves into knots, this serves as metaphor for our inner experience. On the path of stretching, we can never be sure which way is up.

A poet delights in all this. Thwarted expectations—that's the juice of the spiritual journey. That's good poetry! We can step on the mat in a foul mood and finish giddy. We can launch into the asana designed for our physiques and, God knows why, fall flat on our faces. Whenever the path of stretching veers from reason, we invoke the poet who doesn't know any better, who watches the world with wonder, who still believes a sunrise is worth a poem because every sunrise is the first sunrise on earth.

On the path of stretching, we become both scientist and poet. We step on the yoga mat ready for anything and open to everything. We watch carefully. We take note, delighting in surprises. We breathe deep and finish breathless.

Both scientists and poets begin by learning proper form. Today's yoga world presents a dizzying array of asanas, sequences and styles. One could wander forever, sampling every new stretch. Don't play the field for too long. The science and poetry of stretching take place once our bodies learn the poses. Not our minds. Our bodies. The key is repetition. When we have to remember what comes next, unsure of the pose or the sequence, we remain at the surface of the asana. We can't observe the vast detail of our inner world or delight in its unfolding mystery if we nervously wonder where next to place our foot.

On a practical level, this means picking a teacher, a studio, or even a YouTube video and sticking with it. Initially, I chose Bikram Yoga and practiced at the same studio, with the same cadre of teachers, every day.

Even with this consistency, it took a few months before my body knew the asanas. It took a year before I saw something that blew my mind.

You certainly don't need to choose Bikram Yoga, though I've found this to be a wonderful series for those new to the path of stretch. In fact, you don't need to choose Hatha Yoga at all, if you find another form of physical practice, such as Ashtanga Yoga, Pilates, Feldenkrais or Tai Chi, more amenable. Whatever the discipline, choose a practice that permits you to move slowly, carefully, ever connected with breath and ever mindful of the feedback your body provides.

As we progress in our practice, whatever our practice, our spines will lengthen. The crowns of our heads will grow closer to the sky. We will infuse the twisting tubes of our bodies with space and breath and explode into bliss. We'll have days when we exit the studio and float to our cars, humming and high. Stretching can feel that good.

On the path of stretching, we will need principles to anchor us to earth. Without these lifelines, we may find ourselves forgetting our original intention. We started stretching to find God. Now we're stretching to get high. Originally, we oriented ourselves toward the mountain. Now we're happy here in the valley, smiling in our stretch pants, eager for the next fix.

A few key yogic principles will tether us, keeping us honest and pointing us in the right direction. They will focus our minds and provide metrics for our practice. Anchored in these principles, we can let the good times ebb and flow, enjoying the sweeter moments and shrugging off the harder sessions. Our practice won't depend on temperamental emotional feedback. Regardless of how we feel, we simply align ourselves again and again with these principles, moving steadily up the mountain.

I learned to ground my practice through yogic principles when I trained with a soft-spoken, fifty-something, reclusive yogi named Tony Sanchez. I hadn't intended to study with Tony. Two years after my first Bikram class, I wanted to join the ranks as a Bikram teacher myself. The teacher certification process required an eleven-thousand-dollar check and nine weeks of eight a.m. to midnight training, the training held at a B-grade hotel on the periphery of the Los Angeles airport, overseen by Bikram Choudhury himself.

The minute I declared my intention to enroll, various teachers at the Bikram studio started preparing me for what I would encounter. Forget the standard 105-degree heat. Bikram teachers are forged by fire. Teacher training, I was told, stuffed four hundred trainees into the hotel's converted ballroom for twice-daily classes held in upward of 120 degrees. Choudhury would teach many of these, barking and taunting while perched on a high stage under his own personal air-conditioning vent. Students showed up the first week enthusiastic and idealistic, eager recruits for the yoga revolution. Training broke them. They sobbed and retched. They dragged one another from the battlefield, dosing the wounded with homemade electrolyte concoctions and Trader Joe's energy bars. Nine weeks later, Choudhury would knight a dehydrated army of hard-bodied, spandex-clad, beaming believers.

I'll admit—I was intimidated, both by the tales of hazing and the eleven-thousand-dollar price tag. But I loved the yoga. Bikram teacher training felt preordained, a natural stepping-stone on my mountain ascent. Still a pulpit rabbi in Boston, I rehearsed my pitch to the synagogue board. I would take a nine-week mini-sabbatical, complete the training, and return a yogi-rabbi extraordinaire. The board could then capitalize on this quirky blend of lox and bagels meets dal and rice. Most Jews in Boston had never heard of our tiny hamlet of a temple. Through a coordinated press release and open-to-the-public yoga classes, we'd become a center for Jewish spirituality, a back-bending rabbi at the helm.

Just as I rounded the corner on two years of yoga practice and started filling out the Bikram Yoga Teacher Training application, I picked up a new book on yoga written by another Bikram devotee. Sara and I devoured the book, arguing each night over whose turn it was with the Kindle.

The book, filled with dramatic tales of Bikram Yoga Teacher Training, confirmed many of the reports I'd already gathered. At the end of the book, however, the author turned his attention from Bikram Choudhury and Bikram Yoga to a yogi by the name of Tony Sanchez. Tony had studied with Bikram in the late 1970s and early 1980s. He then left Bikram's orbit and founded his own yoga school in San Francisco. Yet, in 2005, just as Tony's status as a guru began to bloom, he disappeared. He and his wife Sandy packed their car, drove south and didn't stop until they arrived in Los Cabos. So began Tony's decade of isolation. He practiced yoga all day, every day, alone on his living room floor. When he emerged, he invited a handful of Bikram instructors down to Los Cabos for a series of informal workshops, teaching them his own methodology of yoga practice and instruction.

After reading the author's description of this brilliant, reclusive yogi, gently dispensing wisdom from the beaches of Baja, I knew I had to study with him. I located Tony's bare-bones website and emailed him. Sandy wrote back. Sure, she told me, I could train with Tony. He was holding a couple of teacher trainings the following year in Los Cabos, certifying teachers, not in Bikram Yoga, but in the lineage of Hatha Yoga taught by Bikram's guru, Bishnu Charan Ghosh.

For the next year, I split my yoga practice between classes at the Bikram studio and sessions at home using a video from Tony's website. The following December, I flew to Los Cabos, joining thirty other students, mostly Bikram-trained teachers, many of us clad in T-shirts advertising various Bikram studios across the country. Tony led every aspect of training, guiding us through two yoga sessions a day interspersed with lectures, Q&As and posture clinics. Throughout our two weeks together, he familiarized us with the key yogic principles needed for healthy, productive and sustainable practice, languidly voicing these principles in his heavily accented English.

To ensure we stretched in the right direction, we first needed the principle of breath. In yoga practice, the breath should remain steady, gentle, deep and relaxed. Above all, we must notice the breath, cleaving to it and letting it guide us through our practice. As a spiritual cross-trainer, I'd witnessed the blessing of breath in meditation practice, how inhalation and exhalation brought my busy mind and buzzing body home. Now, on the stretching path, Tony encouraged us to adopt a similar reverence, anchoring our awareness to the breath before, during and after each asana.

As we ground our practice with each breath, Tony continued, we must also employ a second point of focus: the spine. With every pose, we ask ourselves: What is the spine doing in this pose? Is the spine opening in the front and compressing in the back, or vice versa? Is the spine lengthening? Or bending laterally right or left? Or twisting? As the literal and figurative backbone of our practice, the spine should become our obsession.

I had at least some experience connecting with breath. Focusing on the spine, however, proved more difficult. In the middle of a tough asana, I wanted to focus on my limbs and joints. My hips groaned in *Tadasana,* Tree Pose, so I directed my energy to these squeaky wheels, willing my hips to open more and more. Wasn't it my job in *Tadasana* to chisel away the mass of connective tissue binding femur to ilium? Didn't yoga teachers call *Tadasana* a "hip-opener" for this very reason?

No, Tony explained, in yoga, there's really no such thing as a "hip-opener." Sure, some asanas help increase the flexibility of our hip joints. Ultimately, though, every exercise is a spinal exercise. We're not stretching to have flexible hips. Or tight abs. We're not stretching to be able to touch our toes. We're stretching to find self-realization. And to find self-realization, to kiss the cosmos, we need to heal. We need to relax and release the coil of nerves that cling to our spines. When we initiate each movement from the spine, for the spine, with the spine, we utilize the pose to massage our nervous system.

Another pose, *Paschimottanasana,* found us bending at the waist, placing our hands behind our ankles and sandwiching upper body to lower body. Each time I hung upside down like this, blood collecting in my brain pan, my hamstrings greeted me with adamant howls of resistance. Previously, I had answered their call with redoubled effort, trying my hardest to straighten my legs. Now, however, I nodded to my hamstrings and then bid them adieu, focusing once more on the spine and extending my vertebral column closer and closer to the floor. Time and gravity had robbed my spine of its natural buoyancy. In *Paschimottanasana* I reversed the process, creating space for nerves to enter and exit, for fluid and nutrients to circulate, for energy to flow.

Of course, by doing so, my hamstrings stretched (much to their chagrin). As a by-product of spinal work, my joints loosened, abdominals tightened, circulation improved, blood pressure dropped and energy soared. Changing my focus didn't mute yoga's effects. Focusing on the spine ensured a safe and sustainable stretch. Rather than working from the outside in, rather than placing the cart before the horse by exerting force through limbs and joints, which produced a higher risk of imbalance and injury, Tony encouraged us to move from the core outward, the spine initiating each movement and driving every pose.

The third essential principle was alignment. In yoga, we needed to align our wild, ungainly bodies with the three-dimensional planes of space. "Practice extending your bodies through an invisible grid," Tony explained. With every pose, we should adjust our bodies to match the lines of this grid, asking questions like: Are my hips aligned with the horizontal plane, parallel to the ground, or is one hip slightly higher than the other? When I bend forward to touch my toes, do I lean to the right or left, or am I aligned and balanced? "Let the planes of space be your teachers," Tony continued. Good teachers point us in the right direction. Working with the principles of alignment would do the same.

Working to align our bodies with the planes of space pushes us into uncharted territory. We challenge the body's status quo. Each of us has adopted imbalances in the body, preferring the right or left hand or, when sitting, habitually leaning on one elbow and not the other.

Decades of preference mold us into imbalanced beings, some parts of the body strong and flexible, other parts stiff and weak. Practicing with alignment never eradicates imbalance completely, but again, my mother's maxim: "Have high hopes and low expectations." We don't point toward balance with the expectation we will ever arrive. Our high hopes, our dreams of perfection, show us where to place our next imperfect step. As we do, muscles and joints long forgotten receive the movement, the blood flow and the oxygen they need to heal.

As we stretched with Tony, directing our practice with these three principles of breath, spine, and alignment, our bodies hurt. By introducing significant movement into areas with significant resistance, we tugged at muscle and bone long encased in connective tissue, uncovering storehouses of pain. Our bodies had done their job, binding underused tissue together for protection and efficiency. Now we had shown up with a chisel and blowtorch, hacking away at our body's equilibrium. The body resented this intrusion. It let us know with every ache.

On the path of stretching, coming to terms with pain on the mat will help us come to terms with pain on our search. Seeking the light can be painful. Every path to God hurts. Silence, stretching, and song illuminate the thousand traumas obscuring our souls. We house these traumas in our very cells. When we open our creaky, cobwebbed shutters, letting light into the room, we don't have to view the resulting pain as a problem to be avoided. Pain is a natural by-product of the birth of freedom from slavery. Pain tells us we're pointed in the right direction.

When we stop running from pain, when we turn into the storm, we need to do so slowly and carefully. Tony would tell us to "dip our toes into the ocean of pain" and then very slowly, millimeter by millimeter, edge deeper into the water. When more pain appears—Pause. Breathe. Relax. Go a millimeter deeper, to a new frontier of resistance. Then—Pause. Breathe. Relax.

By moving slowly in yoga, we give our muscles time and space—necessary components for relaxation. Physiologically, muscles contain sensory receptors called spindles. Spindles detect the depth of a stretch, activating motoneurons in the muscle to resist a potentially dangerous stretch. Spindles respond not only to the depth of a stretch, but to its velocity. They're the curmudgeons in the congregation. If we want things to change, we need to sneak up on these spindles, going very, very, *very* slowly. When we edge forward slowly, they sit back in their seats and relax, virtually unaware that the earth shifts beneath.

One of my favorite Bikram teachers, who frequently began her classes with stories of beer-and-bacon binges the night before, once described this process with a helpful metaphor. She had been out on a camping trip, sitting by the fire with a beer in one hand and a skewered marshmallow in the other, when she turned to see a raccoon just a few feet away. What should she do? If she sat absolutely still, the raccoon would rummage through her food. If she jumped up, the frightened animal might attack. Rather than choose either option, she started backing away in slow motion, millimeter by millimeter. Once out of range, she then clattered some pots and pans and sent the bandit running for the woods. "When you stretch," she concluded, "pretend you've got a raccoon a few feet away."

Some pain will indicate growth and some pain will warn us of danger. We need to know the difference. Iyengar writes that the pain we need is "a gradual lengthening and strengthening feeling" while the pain we must avoid is "a sharp and sudden cautionary feeling." When you stretch, if you feel pain and don't like it, if you wish you weren't feeling it, that's not a reason to back off. That's the work. However, if the pain frightens you, if your gut tells you that something is wrong, reverse out of the asana until the pain subsides.

On the path of silence, we spiritual cross-trainers struggle to sit still. Now, on the path of stretching, we may find it hard to move. Maybe we're tired. Maybe the asana hurts. Or the whole practice today isn't going well. It's just not our day. On the path of stretching, as we work with pain, we may need a little help staying in the game.

As Tony led us trainees through a difficult posture series, our joints squealing, our brows furrowed, he would casually add an extra direction to his teaching. He'd be saying something like, "Bring your hips down on your heels. Bring your arms over your head. Palms together . . ." and then he'd slip in the line, "Bring the corners of your mouth to your ears."

Each time I heard that line, I couldn't help it—I grinned big and bright. It's not that my knees stopped hurting. It's not that my tight hips finally released. I hadn't conquered a long sought-after goal. Nor did I understand my life any better than a moment earlier. No, the bearded guy sitting on his heels, arms raised above his head, sweaty and smiling, was still messy old me. At the same time, when Tony reminded us to smile, when the corners of our mouths dutifully obeyed, everything changed. We felt lighter. We regained a sense of hope, of promise, of the very reason we spent so many hours on the mat. *Joy*—the final ingredient—took our stretch from arduous chore to devotional dance.

This attitude of joy mirrors the "No big deal" attitude we invoked in meditation. In fact, as spiritual cross-trainers, we're welcome to hum this same mantra of "No big deal" on the yoga mat. No matter what we think is going on in a given stretch, no matter how triumphant or tragic, we can think "No big deal" and just keep going. The wisdom of "No big deal" buffers us from pride and resignation. Yesterday we rocked a back bend. *No big deal.* Today we can't touch our forehead to our knee, even though we've done it a thousand times before. *No big deal.* We feel inspired and explosive on the mat. *No big deal.* We feel pathetic and incompetent and downright embarrassed. *No big deal.* We can feel what we feel. We can think what we think. Then we can let it all go and return to the ever-present, non-judgmental, monotonous, miraculous breath.

When we practice joyfully, treating the peaks and valleys with equanimity, smiling through it all, our stretching becomes a celebration. On days when we drift through a sea of striving, our dance to the Creator turned desperate performance, our bright eyes turned fierce, we can remember Tony's wise instruction: "Bring the corners of your mouth to your ears." Giggling, grinning, our smile brings us back home. Back to the mat. Back to our messy old selves. Back to celebrating this glorious, not-ready-for-primetime, nonetheless beautiful life.

THE SUMMIT OF LIGHT

Light.

Light counters the heavy. On our search for God, we move through every stretch with a light heart. Like a child beholding a wonderfully mundane adventure, we raise our eyebrows. We smile. We stretch with a light heart, our practice becoming a dance.

Light.

Light banishes the dark. Each stretch opens wounds and flushes scar tissue. We start to see what we could not see before. We cannot search for the Source only in the universe beyond our skin. We need to take our search to the cellular terrain. Stretching illuminates our inner world. If we're blessed, we may find our cells smudged with the telltale fingerprints of God.

Deep illumination takes time. I began a serious yoga practice in the darkest days of December. Three, four, sometimes five times a week, for ninety minutes a class, I stretched. Every month, I felt better than the month before. I lost weight. I stopped smoking. I ate better. But I didn't see anything inside.

A year passed. The following winter, during an otherwise forgettable class on an otherwise forgettable morning, I noticed an odd sensation. Or lack thereof. Compared with the right side of my body, the sensations on my left side felt muted, as if the nerves running through my left hemisphere were wrapped in foam. This proved especially true for certain parts of the left side of the body, especially my left knee, hip, elbow, shoulder and jaw.

I hadn't injured myself. This wasn't a stroke. No, the weakened transmission on my left side felt altogether familiar. I had lived with this imbalance for decades. The imbalance had eluded me because, until now, the imbalance lived in the dark, undiscovered territory of my tissue. A year of stretching had uncovered layer upon layer of subtle physiology. Finally, one morning, another layer peeled away to reveal what I could not have noticed before.

Once I discovered this lack of sensation in my left side, it didn't take great powers of intellect to deduce its origins. Yes, I'm right-handed, and this preference alone would lead to a stronger right side. This was just the beginning. From early childhood, the right side of my body has flourished while my left side, time and time again, has been twisted and torn. Such unfair treatment began at the age of six. My Suzuki violin teacher, handing me a cardboard violin at my first lesson, instructed me in the proper positioning of said cardboard between left shoulder and left jaw. Step one: place the violin on the left shoulder. Step two: lift the chin, tensing the jaw and neck muscles. Step three: bring the lifted chin over to the left, so that the chin and left jaw can compress the base of the violin onto the left shoulder. Step four: hold that position, neck and jaw muscles simultaneously extending and twisting.

If done correctly, this shoulder-jaw sandwich stabilizes the violin, freeing the left hand to dance unburdened over the strings. If done correctly over many years, this shoulder-jaw sandwich reshapes the very fabric of a student's muscle and skeletal tissue—all at an angle. Like a tree growing next to a fence, its trunk bending, folding and twisting against the unyielding barrier, my neck and jaw spent the next decade growing around my violin. By the time I put the violin away, swapping it for the piano at age sixteen, the violin had left its indelible mark.

The assault on my left side continued. Three years after beginning violin, I climbed a tree in my grandparents' backyard, fell ten feet and landed on my left arm. I don't remember screaming, though my parents, grandparents and grandparents' neighbors certainly do. I do remember looking at my left arm and thinking, "Wow, it looks like the letter *s*." My elbow had been dislocated and broken in three places. My wrist had been dislocated and broken in two places. The doctors also discovered that I had damaged the growth plate in my elbow. I had no idea what that meant. From the look of ever-growing concern on my parents' faces, however, I realized I wouldn't merely get to show up in school the following week with a cool cast to sign and an elaborate tale to tell. Doctors began throwing around words like "surgery" and "years to recover." No, this would not be a fun story to tell.

I underwent surgery, followed by many months of doctor visits and recuperation. I even made it into a medical journal and got to stand up in front of a conference of visiting doctors, my own doctor projecting X-rays on a screen behind us while proudly displaying my repaired arm for all to see. Thankfully, the breaks and the growth plate healed. To my doctor's amazement, I recovered 99 percent of the range of motion in my elbow, due in no small part to the following summer's waterskiing, where the towrope's pull on my extended arms helped to straighten and strengthen the elbow. Nevertheless, my left side had once more been marked.

Next, we arrive at the hot dog cart fiasco. Rather than returning to summer camp after ninth grade, I found a job running a hot dog cart in front of an office building in downtown Milwaukee. No doubt violating countless labor laws, our boss required us to push our carts up a ramp into the back of an enclosed truck and then to stand with the carts as the truck barreled toward our drop-off points. Each time the back opened to let one of us out, we vendors squinted into the sunlight and enjoyed a few precious gulps of fresh air.

Upon reaching my corner one morning, I wheeled my hot dog cart down the truck's ramp and then hopped back into the truck to retrieve a large plastic bucket of condiments. As I walked back down the ramp, sauerkraut and relish in tow, I slipped and fell over the side of the ramp to the street below. I broke my fall, you guessed it, with my left hand, breaking my left wrist.

Finally, there's the most recent chapter of left-side degradation: tearing the cartilage of my left knee while meditating. As a cavalier, college-aged Zen student, the personal Zen koan I chose to explore during meditation was, "If my knees hurt enough to scream, will I make a sound?" After one such excruciatingly painful meditation retreat at a Zen Center in Greenwich Village, I returned to school, went jogging and felt a piercing pain in my left knee. A few cycles of rest, ice, compression, and elevation failed to do the trick, so I hobbled to an orthopedist. He informed me that I had torn my left knee's medial meniscus. Surgery was optional, but if I wanted a pain-free knee, I'd need to go under the knife.

Time heals. If we're inattentive to that healing process, however, if we assume that the injuries of the past will get washed away with the tide, time heals with duct tape and string. A broken body will cobble together a new normal, and for a while, this may suffice. Following two decades of left-side breaks and tears, for instance, I enjoyed a decade and a half of trauma-free existence. I maintained an active lifestyle, bounding through city streets, sweating on elliptical machines and chasing after children (my own). I even spent a year in a physical theatre conservatory, testing my body's strength and flexibility with acrobatics, yoga and dance. Through it all, both hemispheres of my body, left and right, remained relatively pain free. Time, I assumed, had done its job. Time had healed.

A year on the yoga mat pulled back the curtain on my outwardly functional left side. The path of stretching heightened the sensitivity of my nervous system. For the first time, I sensed the mounds of scar tissue that compromised mobility on my left side. I noticed the lack of sensation on the left side of my body in comparison with the right. A year of yoga under my belt and I had arrived at my first big climb.

So began a second year of stretching. On the mat, I started paying careful attention to the left side of my body. If the bold, boisterous right side wished to plunge deeper into a pose, I first checked in with the left. What did I feel there? Was the left a passive participant or an equally engaged partner? If the left side had indeed relinquished all autonomy to the dominant right, if the left offered little sensory feedback, a sign of disengaged muscles, tendons, and nerves, I backed off, waited, and began the stretch again. Slowly. With as much patience as I could muster. Almost always, this second try brought the left side off the sidelines and into the game.

Bikram Yoga draws in competitive types. Bikram Choudhury was a yoga competitor himself, India's national champion many times over, before wandering to the West. The language and mood of a Bikram Yoga class, the encouragement to stretch with "English bulldog determination and Bengal tiger strength," lifts bulldog- and tiger-types like me into an eyes blazing, nostrils flaring, chest heaving trance.

My first year of practice, I fought for the deep, delicious asana. I wasn't trying to be the best yogi in the room. I was trying to be the best yogi in the world. And lucky for me, my flat feet, tight hips and tenaciously faithful love handles not withstanding, the good Lord blessed me with an unusually flexible back. Whenever we hit the back bends in class, I fed on a steady stream of "nice, Ben" and "excellent one, Ben" from my instructors. The studio owner even stopped class one morning and asked me to demonstrate. *Was it a sign?* I thought during that first year. *Was yoga my true calling?* Perhaps the status and celebrity for which I'd always yearned was buried in the very discs of my spine, my vertebrae the winning lottery tickets for a life elevated above the mundane.

In my second year, I started really listening to my left side, my many-times-broken, passive, not-exactly-healed left side. I backed off on each stretch until my left side engaged. As I did so, I also backed off from my dream of yogic stardom. Take the asana *Dandayamana Dhanurasana,* otherwise known as Standing Bow Pose. In Standing Bow, the practitioner stands on one leg with the other leg folded behind, the foot held behind the butt with one hand. With this folded leg, the yogi kicks back until the torso is parallel to the floor. The once-folded leg, still held in the hand, lifts toward the ceiling, while the other arm reaches forward toward the front of the room. In its final expression, Standing Bow brings the body into the standing splits.

I wasn't in the splits, not by a long shot, but by the end of my first year of yoga practice, I was far enough to get teachers excited, to feed on their praise and imagine the spot-lit future to which it would lead. Honoring my ne'er-do-well left side, however, forced me to take a long, hard look at Standing Bow. As I launched into this signature pose, the muscles in my left leg and hip failed to engage. My right leg overcompensated, wrenching my hips far out of alignment. My shoulders, ever strong and eager, sensed the general breakdown and flexed to pull my leg and spine deeper into the pose. From afar, the pose looked good. In actuality, it was a real mess. I had made Standing Bow look good at the expense of doing it right.

In year two, I began to back off. I practiced Standing Bow correctly, adhering to form and alignment at the expense of depth. Now, the mirrors no longer reflected a super-yogi on the road to perfection. They revealed a second-year student appropriately struggling with a challenging asana. With these adjustments, teacher superlatives grew sparse. I received praise at about the same rate as the students huffing and puffing around me.

I've wanted to be special since the very birth of my ego. Take away fame and notoriety, and the schematics of my identity collapse. In that second year of practice, as I refocused from attention received to integrity achieved, I struggled with my now aimless ambition. Quitting praise cold turkey left me edgy. I needed some yogic methadone, an earthly goal to help me once more feel special on the mat.

So I decided to trick myself. *You want to be special, Ben? Fine. Only we're going to adjust the metrics. A super-yogi is no longer one who receives attention and praise. From now on, a super-yogi is one who practices with devotion. A super-yogi devotes himself to form, body, and breath. A super-yogi infuses every asana with gentleness and joy. You want to know if you're doing well? If you spend a class yearning for praise and strong-arming mind and body to deliver on ego's demands, you blew it. Better luck next time. If, on the other hand, the class felt like an offering, a prayer—you've taken one more step toward super-yogi stardom.*

During the months that followed, I stayed committed to these revised criteria. I had a few good classes, a few bad classes and plenty in between. Super-yogi moments, though rare, kept me in the game.

During one memorable session, I lay down at the end of class in *Savasana,* or Corpse Pose. I closed my eyes and brought my attention to the breath flowing quickly in and out of my nose. I felt my body settle deeper and deeper into the mat.

Then, suddenly, I was no longer in the studio. I was standing in a medium-sized office, furnished with a wide, imposing desk, meeting chairs and couch. On all sides, large, leather-bound tomes lined the walls. On top of the desk sat a commemorative gavel and some framed photographs—photographs of my parents, my brother and me.

As a child, I had spent many hours in this book-lined sanctuary, watching my father enter and exit in his long black robes. Following my fall from the tree and the surgery that followed, I had spent two weeks in this office before the doctors allowed me to return to school. Every morning, my dad would drive us to the courthouse, my arm bound in cast and sling, my eyes staring out the window at the morning's freeway traffic. We'd then make our way through long, freshly waxed courthouse hallways; the barrel-chested bailiffs, briefcase-toting lawyers and depressed defendants greeting my father with, "Mornin' Judge." Eventually, we'd arrive at a locked, unmarked door which opened into my father's chambers. I'd settle on the couch with the previous day's homework, sent home by my teachers, while my father would don his robes and pass through another door, entering his courtroom.

I spent those weeks convalescing in unexpressed terror. The doctors seemed cautiously optimistic about my recovery, but no one had ever seen a break quite like this. No one, not the doctors, not my parents, could predict the end of this story. Possibilities ranged from complete recovery to a left arm visually stunted and physically compromised. Life as I knew it may have ended. As my father sentenced convicts in the courtroom next door, I felt myself sentenced in those chambers, a prisoner to an injury that might never heal.

Back in these chambers now, I looked from couch to books to desk to door, tracing the architecture of my childhood anxiety. Eventually, my eyes circled back to the couch. There, in front of me, stood my nine-year-old self. Plaster encased his left arm from fingers to bicep, the ugly apparatus held to his chest with a sling. Dark circles cradled worried eyes pleading for some assurance. He didn't know what was going to happen. He was afraid.

"Ben," I heard myself say, "it's going to be okay. You're going to get better. Your arm is going to heal. Trust me. You are going to be okay."

I opened my eyes. Most of the class had exited the yoga studio. Slowly, I turned to one side, got to my feet, and rolled up my yoga mat. Then I headed for the showers.

According to the Jewish mystical tradition of Kabbalah, God created the universe with divine light. God took this light and hid it deep within every atom. To know God, the Kabbalists taught, to connect with the Creator, one must search for this light. We can search for it in the eyes of another. We can uncover it in the objects of our world, from the leaves of trees to the passing clouds to even the discarded can by the side of the road. The external appearance of things is an illusion. A trick of the light. When we gaze deeply, we will see a divine spark as rich and bright as a thousand suns.

The infinite chambers of our body contain this light. When we embark on the path of stretching, we challenge the body to open, to tell its secrets and to reveal its light. For a long time, we may see nothing at all. Then, perhaps on a winter morning when we least expect it, we may see something. We may discover ancient hieroglyphics etched in bone, their convolutions tracing the hurt that makes us human. God's light has begun to illuminate our sad, sweet story.

On the search for God, this network of wounds narrates where we've been. Our beautiful, broken bodies also map where we must go. To find the light, we'll need to loosen our stiff necks. We'll need to relax all the way to our bones. We'll need to heal. Then the light of God will shine from our deepest cells out beyond our skin. We won't even need to search for God. With a beacon that bright, God will come searching for us.

PART III:
SONG

THE VALLEY OF SHAME

Silence penetrates the mind. Stretching burrows through bone. Layer upon layer, we peel the onion, stinging with tears. As spiritual cross-trainers climbing that impossible mountain, we can grow dreadfully serious. We need a song.

The Psalmist observed: *The whole world is singing to God* (Ps. 66:4). On the path of song, we wake up to this. Close your eyes right now and listen. What do you hear? *Listen.* The clink of glasses. The rumble of the train. The soft hum of the humidifier. Grass rustling in wind. Cell phones ringing. Two women in conversation, each humming "mm-hmm" to one another. *The whole world is singing to God.* Every moment Creation sings.

We sing to join the chorus. When we embark on the path of song, we smudge our lonely outlines and blend into the watercolor surrounding us. The path of song launches us through our private atmosphere to the galaxy beyond. Song takes the breath, the breath that has so dutifully anchored us on the meditation cushion and the yoga mat, and sends it out. Out of our lungs. Out of our mouths. Out beyond our borders. To somewhere else. To someone else. To ears not our own. The path of song elevates the tension entangling us, lifts it upon the breath and sends it away. We offer our joy and our pain, our triumph and our tragedy, to one another.

Song turns the invisible breath into a precious gift. Every one of us has heard another's voice in a moment of seemingly impenetrable fear and, ears filled with the resonant breath of another, found our own breath again. Every one of us has felt our heart open by a melody's kind touch. Imagine how God must feel, receiving such a gift. Imagine how much closer we will come to our Creator when we arrive bearing an offering so sweet.

Sing to God a new song (Ps. 96:1), writes the Psalmist. We can search for God in silence, ears attuned to God's voice. We can stretch our way to the holy mountain, nerves channeling God's light. As spiritual cross-trainers, however, we employ yet another strategy. We ascend by yet another path. We listen for the voice, we look for the light, and then, in song, we call out. We beckon God from hiding with our offering of song.

As spiritual cross-trainers, we don't mind how the paths of meditation and song, silent breath and sounding voice, appear to contradict. We bask in silence, then we rise up singing. We fly high on song, then sit down, still and quiet. We keep dancing up God's mountain, accompanied by notes and rests. We're delighted to bounce from one path to another, watching the breath transform from a gentle breeze to a storm of sound to a gentle breeze once more. The Jewish mystics, on their own search for God, understood the power and potency of song. Beginning in the sixteenth century, fraternities of mystics gathered every Friday evening in the fields around Tzfat, a tiny village in Israel's Galilee. The sun had just settled below the horizon, initiating the sky's slow bleed from blue to gray. The mystics murmured their late afternoon prayers, occasional moments of unison interrupting cacophonous devotions.

Then, cozy in the soft haze of twilight, eyes gazing south to the golden city of Jerusalem, the mystics began to sing. Psalm after psalm poured forth, rising on ancient melodies. "Sing to God a new song," they chanted. "The whole world is singing to God," they shouted. "Shake off the dust and arise!" they whooped and howled. With each line of ancient scripture, their voices grew in volume and intensity, until finally, the huddled mass exploded into movement. Grown men became boisterous boys, gripping one another's shoulders, spinning round and round. As they danced, eyes alight, chests heaving, hearts thumping, stars began to pierce the darkened sky. They opened their arms, bowed low and invited the Sabbath Queen to enter, singing "come my bride, come my bride." Then, grabbing each other arm in arm, they danced down the hillside to their homes. The holy Sabbath had arrived.

My first exposure to this style of Sabbath Eve celebration came three hundred kilometers south and four hundred years later. I had just moved to the Israeli town of Arad. That first Friday night, as I sat in a dusty, white-walled classroom, a prayer book filled with unintelligible Hebrew resting open in my lap, I kept wiping my eyes and running my fingers down the bridge of my nose. My head throbbed, protesting the past week's Hebrew immersion classes. Just a few hours' drive south of the Galilee, I felt a million miles from anything resembling Tzfat.

Around me, equally exhausted, slumped a ragtag group of Jewish twenty-something ex-pats. Many had left families, jobs, and schools in America to emigrate to Israel—the Hebrew immersion classes a vital first step toward citizenship. A few others had booked return flights, regarding the year in Israel as a "gap year" between undergraduate studies and grown-up life. I fit into this second category. In the two years since college graduation, I'd crashed and burned at the Zen Center, wandered dazed and confused back home in Milwaukee, and then, as you will soon see, found my way out west, dancing and dodging tennis balls in the land of the clowns.

I approached this year in Arad as a hoop to jump through on my way to rabbinical school. A month earlier, while touring a seminary in the states, the dean of admissions had explained to me that I needed a year of Hebrew immersion before my application would be considered. "Go to Israel," he commanded.

That was September 10, 2001. The next morning, I sat in on a class at the seminary titled, "Religious Extremism." Midway through the professor's lecture, someone burst into the classroom, telling us that a plane had struck the World Trade Center. As America rubbed its tearful eyes and gathered its feral rage, as the world waited for the next cataclysmic shoe to drop, I packed my bags for Arad.

I had enrolled in the World Union of Jewish Students Institute, known by its acronym WUJS (pronounced by Westerners as "woo-jus" and by Israelis as "voo-jus"). WUJS students lived and studied in an immigrant absorption center on the outskirts of Arad. Still, silent desert surrounded the center on three sides, blowing tumbleweeds past the center's front gate. I shared a cold, stark room with a fellow twenty-something American. When he dropped out a few months into the program, he left me a choice of two government-issue, metal-springed, thin-mattressed beds. On the floors above and below lived immigrants from Russia, Brazil, Ethiopia, and other diverse points on the globe. Many of the Ethiopians had never seen an elevator. As I held the doors open, their more experienced counterparts reassured these new arrivals, in their native Amharic, that they could safely enter our miraculous levitating cube.

Smack in the middle of our assembled lot this Friday evening, glancing at his watch and readjusting a yarmulke that forever migrated down the side of his head, stood Rabbi Aubrey Isaacs. Aubrey, and he insisted we call him "Aubrey," served as WUJS's rabbi-in-residence. A short, disheveled, Scottish Jew who had moved to Israel in his teens,

Aubrey frequently hurried through the absorption center's hallways in much the same manner as Arad's tumbleweeds—bouncing and bumping along, scraps of paper falling from his pockets, one or two of his children clinging to the ritual fringes of his undershirt. I loved Aubrey. He loved us, too. He didn't care that many of us had dropped out of Jewish life long ago, or if we had ever participated at all. He didn't mind our irreverence, our ignorance, the impossible challenge we presented to even the best of Jewish educators. Whatever our back-stories, however we'd made our way to the Holy Land, he celebrated our choice to join him in the desert.

At the helm that first Friday night, Aubrey gave no formal intro-duction. Instead, he mounted the podium, hunched over his prayer book, and began to sing. Psalm after psalm exploded from his thin whine of a voice, his body swaying to and fro. Aubrey sang as if sur-rounded, not by our group of silent, slack-jawed misfits, but by Tzfat's ancient mystics. He meant every word. He stood in that shitty little room, in that shitty little town, and transported us to the Galilean hills.

At the climax of the service, sweating and shouting, Aubrey turned to us, held out his hands and yanked each of us into an expanding circle of whirling bodies. We danced round and round, eyes wide, hearts pounding. We stopped singing Hebrew lyrics, which only a few of us knew, and started shouting "Yai yai yai!" The collective sound shook our bones. When one of us unraveled and collapsed into a chair, giggling and grinning, others pulled him back into the circle.

My head no longer hurt. I had forgotten all about the past week's struggles with Hebrew. I drifted joyfully through a sea of song. I looked up past the absorption center's fluorescent lights and beheld Tzfat's starry sky. I looked to my left and right, and for a brief, wonderful moment, I saw my brothers. The holy Sabbath had indeed arrived.

Over the next decade, first as a rabbinical student and then as an ordained rabbi, Aubrey's song became my sheet music, his soul-ful swaying, the steps I danced. When leading services, I'd prepare by approaching the podium and wrapping my billowing prayer shawl over my head, shoulders and back. Caressed by the shawl's comforting white, alone for a rare and precious moment, I'd imagine my ancestors gathering in the hills. Unfurling the shawl, I'd hold to that imagined horizon. Then our song would begin.

When, almost a decade after my year in Arad, I arrived in Boston, hired by a small congregation as their senior rabbi, the synagogue celebrated our first Friday night together by holding services outdoors. Hundreds came to worship under the stars and to meet the new rabbi and his family. The night was a blur. I led services, belting until I lost my voice, too nervous to notice if anyone joined along. Sara and I spent the next few hours shaking hands and learning names we'd immediately forget. "Did it go okay?" I asked Sara as we walked home that evening. She nodded. The year in Arad dodging tumbleweeds, the six years in seminary buried in books, the two years as an assistant rabbi in the DC suburbs—it had all paid off. We had arrived.

The following Friday, services moved back indoors. I stood at the leader's podium in the synagogue's small chapel, a tall wooden ark housing three Torah scrolls towering before me. A red brick wall surrounded the ark. The bricks ended a small distance from the ceiling, replaced by a thin strip of glass. Through the glass I could see a few tree branches and the evening's blue-gray sky.

Behind me, facing that same brick wall, sat our "Friday Night Regulars," a dozen or so congregants who, rain or shine, come hell or high water, gathered every Friday night to welcome the Sabbath. Each had entered with greetings of "Shabbat Shalom," following this traditional greeting with requisite, weather-related grumblings. Each had then found a seat, the same seat as every week, opened a prayer book and waited for me to begin.

I began as I always began. I wrapped myself in my prayer shawl, recited a private prayer, and thought of Aubrey. Then, buzzing with energy and purpose, eager to inject the spirit of Tzfat into New England veins, I began to sing.

Behind me, I heard nothing. Not a voice. At first, I thought something must be wrong. I looked over my shoulder. Perhaps the entire group had stealthily exited the chapel, eager to get to the after-service schnapps. No, there they were. And to my surprise, I even saw mouths opening and closing, forming the words of the psalms.

What's going on? If their mouths are opening and closing along with mine, why can I only hear my own voice? Am I singing too loudly? I lowered my volume. Nothing. I lowered it even more. *Okay. Now I hear them.* They were singing, sure enough, but with the volume one might use to accompany one's own iPod in a crowded elevator.

Maybe they just need a little encouragement. I looked over my shoulder again, searching for some eye contact, hoping a rabbinic nod-and-smile might draw them out. Some had eyes turned downward. Others looked around the room or out the windows. Everyone looked bored. Disengaged. Their eyes expected nothing.

A year of Friday nights passed like this. I sang and swayed, banging on the table, staring out that sliver of window, hoping we'd edge an inch toward Tzfat. Nothing. Not a peep. I needed help.

At the beginning of year two, I publicized a series of once-a-month Friday night services accompanied by guitar. Attendance jumped from a dozen to one hundred and fifty. We moved services from the red-bricked chapel to a large, bright, window-lined social hall. Many of the Friday Night Regulars grumbled, their long-standing routine upended. Some even protested the new service by gathering in the chapel and leading services themselves. So be it, I thought. They can pray to the brick wall. The rest of us, we're on our way to Tzfat.

I began the service with a few warm, rich chords on the guitar and then launched into our opening song, a classic Hebrew tune familiar to all. The younger kids, sitting cross-legged on the floor up in front, immediately joined in. The hundred and fifty adults behind them smiled big and bright. Heads nodded, feet tapped the beat and mouths opened and closed. Yet, despite our numbers, despite the guitar, the adult voices remained inaudible. The kids sang on their own.

Okay, I thought, *everyone's nervous. We just need to stand up and get the blood flowing.* I jumped to my feet and, guitar strapped around my neck and shoulder, bounced down the aisles. "Let me hear you!" I called between lines of prayer. A few stood up. One or two stepped into the aisles, moving hesitantly. When they noticed no one had joined them, they sat back down. I gave a goofy "oh well" smile and, not knowing what else to do, returned to my seat. Tzfat remained a distant dream.

The following Friday morning, I walked down the hall from my office to the synagogue's preschool, guitar slung to my back. The director of the preschool had invited me to lead the children in a pre-Sabbath song session. I entered the school wing, immediately greeted by my daughter, Avital. She ran to me, clinging to my leg, proudly parading her *Abba* around for all to see.

Together, the children and I sat in a circle, Avital tucking herself between the guitar and my chest. I opened with a classic—*Bim Bam*—a Sabbath song perfectly suited to the preschool set. The song's opening lyric consisted of the meaningless words, *"Bim, bam, bim bim bim bam."* I sang the opening verse, the children staring at me with a mixture of fear and curiosity. "Okay," I said. "Now you know the words. Let me hear you!" I started again. Cautiously, mouths opened. Tiny voices emerged. "One more time!" I called. Our third go-around filled the room with sound. A few even shouted, clapping their hands and bouncing to their feet. Avital giggled and held me tight.

After a few more songs, I wished this enthusiastic congregation a "Shabbat Shalom" and, after surgically removing Avital from my leg with the help of her teachers, headed back to my office. What a contrast—the adult's cool stiffness and the children's joyful noise. With just a little encouragement, the preschoolers had stepped onto the path of song. They had let go. My adult congregants, on the other hand, had responded to this same invitation by tightening their throats, battening down their emotional hatches and sitting silently.

"You've forgotten what it feels like to be in their shoes," Sara said to me that evening. "You know, Ben, there was a time when you were afraid to sing."

It was true. Before my year in Arad, before Aubrey pulled me into the circle and spun the inhibitions right out of me, I participated in prayer as a spectator, my voice silent, my body still. The year before Arad, for instance, I attended a theatre conservatory in the tiny town of McCleary, Washington. I read a lot of Martin Buber in those days; the Jewish philosopher's portrayal of Jewish history as a grand, mythic saga filled me with dreamy ideas of my own role in this epic tale. So one Saturday morning, I grabbed my friend Sean and told him we were headed to services. Sean, while not Jewish, considered himself a card-carrying friend of the tribe. He loved his quirky, intellectual, anxious Jewish friends. He loved Judaism's sensual rituals, full of candles, wine and song. Sean stood out like a sore thumb in Jewish settings, standing well over six feet tall with long, blond hair to his waist, a product of Scottish immigrants mixing with the Native American locals a few generations back. Though he received curious looks every time I brought him to a gathering of God's chosen, he didn't seem to mind.

That Sabbath morning, Sean and I drove thirty minutes east to a tiny synagogue in the city of Olympia. A fellow worshipper wearing an oversized grin walked up to us as we entered the lobby. "Sean!" he called. "How's it going?" Turns out the only stranger at services that morning was me. Sean knew everyone. Of course. Walking with Sean around town felt like playing entourage to a celebrity. A trip to the local co-op for groceries usually involved half an hour of intense discussion between Sean and a fellow supporter of his latest environmental advocacy campaign. I'd drift to the side of the aisle, arms full of organic produce, and wait until they'd confirmed that, yes, big business was evil and, no, all hope was not lost.

After a few more minutes of Sean-style schmoozing in the synagogue lobby, we entered the sanctuary and found our seats. Without a full-time rabbi on staff, the congregation had imported a rabbi from Portland for the weekend. He looked to be in his forties, dressed head to toe in flowing linen, his dark hair, thick beard, and crocheted yarmulke completing his "I'd rather be in Tzfat or at a Grateful Dead show" image.

The rabbi greeted us warmly, giving a few words of introduction to set the mood. Then, guitar already strapped to his chest, he strummed a few chords and began a slow, soulful, Hebrew chant. He closed his eyes. His body swayed. He seemed to feel the chant in his bones.

After a few repetitions, the rabbi opened his eyes and looked out at us in the pews. "Join with me," he called.

The tune was simple, the lyrics just a few Hebrew words, easy to repeat. I opened my mouth. No sound emerged. I wanted to sing, but I felt frozen, a well stopped up with a stone. Shifting awkwardly in their seats, fellow congregants offered equally muted devotions. It seemed like the rabbi would have to go it alone.

Then I heard Sean. Sitting next to me, his back arched, his feet pushing into the floor, he was singing full volume, face turned toward the heavens. The rabbi looked over, smiled, stepped off the podium and moved closer. Together, they sang. The rest of us just stared at these two minstrels, in awe of this unlikely duet. I felt relieved that Sean was singing, taking the pressure off the rest of us, but I also felt ashamed. With all the Jews in attendance, a Scot-Indian was bearing our fire.

Later that day, as we took our customary Saturday afternoon walk through the wooded paths around McCleary, I complimented Sean on his song. "Oh yeah," he answered, "that was just like gospel choir."

As out of place as Sean looked in Jewish settings, it was nothing compared with the year he joined his high school's gospel choir. There, squeezed together with his African-American classmates, Sean discovered the path of song. He witnessed, for the first time, the single stream of his voice joining a bold, beautiful sea of sound. Swaying, clapping, sweating, the choir may as well have been worshiping on the hills of Tzfat. Theirs was a song to God. Theirs was a song to shake off the dust and arise. When Sean had heard the rabbi's chant that morning, his gospel training kicked in. He did what came naturally. He let go.

I didn't. And it wasn't because I couldn't sing. I'd performed in musical theater productions throughout high school and college. I'd taken voice lessons and joined a handful of choirs. I'd sung plenty of songs. Just not the new song. Not the song of my soul. Singing to an audience of hundreds felt just fine. Sitting together with a dozen others and singing a song to God—that terrified me.

On our spiritual cross-training regimen, silence amplifies our internal chatter, stretching traces our tension, and song introduces us again and again to our inhibitions. Unlike preschoolers, who've logged so few hours on earth, who've yet to construct personal parameters for shame, we adults can have a hard time letting go. Maybe we'll raise our voices only in the shower, or at a concert when we imagine no one can hear. Give us enough drinks so we just don't give a damn and, sure, we'll grab the mike at the karaoke bar. The rest of the time, wanting to appear cool and collected, most of us tighten our throats. Even if we imagine ourselves footloose and fancy-free, as I certainly did amid the redwoods of the Pacific Northwest, even if we consider ourselves bold and courageous, the power of song will knock us off this pedestal.

Why? Why would a simple little song inhibit us? What do we fear might happen if we open our mouths and let go?

A lot might happen. A no-holds-barred ballad to God contorts the face. Where else, save in the dentist's chair and the lover's bed, would we open our mouths so wide? On the path of song, we might sweat. Or pant. Or bounce in our seats, goofy as Tigger on his way to Pooh Corner.

As the song builds, as we arch our backs in ecstasy, we may feel a lot like we're out in the open making love. We are. Our song is a lover's song. Our ecstasy begins deep in our belly. If we spend a great deal of energy putting ourselves together, clothes and hair, pressed and coiffured, personae carefully cultivated, the intimacy of song will feel threatening. We're losing our cool, expectorating, vibrating, out of control.

And if we travel far enough on the path of song, we risk triggering something truly transformational. Our own preschooler will emerge. The child in us will leap out and go wild. We do not act like children when we sing. We *become* children when we sing. *Sing to God a new song.* Does this mean we need to throw out our well-worn hymnals, forever singing original compositions? Not necessarily. We can sing a new song by singing new notes; or, more effectively, we can sing a new song by *becoming new ourselves.* We can sing like we're fresh from the womb, new to this earth, releasing with raw, uncultivated abandon. Wild like a child.

Many of us don't want to go there. We feel ashamed of our wild child. Who knows what he or she might do? Growing up in Milwaukee, Wisconsin, Little Ben Shalva couldn't sit still. He had trouble making friends. He spent a lot of time in the corner, or the principal's office, or alone in his room.

I once saw a video of myself at age six. In the video, I sat on the edge of my Hebrew-school teacher's desk, little legs dangling. Rachel, a shy little girl, also in my class, sat by my side. Our teacher, standing out of sight behind the camera, started asking us questions. "Ben, what's your favorite Jewish holiday?" "Christmas!" I shouted, grinning mischievously. "Ben, who is your favorite character in the Torah?" Without hesitation: "Batman!" My teacher wisely moved on. "Rachel," he asked, "what's your favorite holiday?" Rachel began to answer, but I shouted over her, "Say Christmas!" She tried to speak again, but I put my hand over her mouth, launching into an explanation of Batman's noble Semitic heritage.

I hadn't even known this video existed until, years later, our kindergarten teacher showed up with it at our Hebrew-school graduation.

With a sly smile, he simply popped the video in and stood back. Everyone gathered around the screen. Now sixteen years old, I stood between my parents, the now teenage Rachel standing a few feet away. When Rachel and I appeared on screen, I couldn't believe my eyes. *Was that really me? Was I really that crazy?* I looked over at my parents. They wore this strange, slightly amused, slightly traumatized expression on their faces. They didn't say a word. Every once in a while, one of them would glance over at me, meet my eyes and give me a knowing nod.

I watched the footage and laughed and said, "Aww shucks." Inside, however, I detested that little boy. He embarrassed me. He shamed me. Why wouldn't he shut up? Why couldn't he keep it together? I watched that video as Ben the smart and capable. I had my shit together. It had taken close to a decade of painstaking social refinement and academic effort to banish that little boy on the desk. I had buried him. For good. Aside from this video, nothing caused me to confront that pudgy-cheeked, bed-headed, embarrassment of a boy. On the contrary, my teenage persona confirmed his disappearance. Good riddance.

But on a Friday night in Arad, Aubrey pulled me into that whirling circle of song. The centrifugal force of our dance dislodged me from gravity's good sense. I couldn't help myself. I let go. For a few precious moments, I forgot all about Ben the smart and capable. I contorted my face and opened my mouth embarrassingly wide. I panted. I sweat. I looked up to the highest heavens. And the voice that emerged—it belonged to my inner child, my delightful, delight-filled inner child.

On the path of song, guaranteed, we will meet the child within. We will encounter our Peter Pan, the part of our soul that refuses to grow up. We will also run smack into our shame, the shame this child felt when the world said, "You're not worthy of love just as you are." We will dip our toes into shame's primordial pool, into the dark waters out of which, long ago, our ego emerged. Through a liberating but often painful process, the path of song reverse-engineers our identity's construction, letting our child out of its cage.

We may wonder, as spiritual cross-trainers, about our wild child's worth. If we allow this child to sing, will this offering delight the Holy One? Will the Source of Life accept a misfit's devotion? Slowly, song by song, God will give us an answer. We will open our mouths, let go, and watch our loneliness disappear. What we've hidden completes us. We feel at peace, enveloped in divine embrace. The Holy One was waiting for this child. The Creator has picked us up. We're swinging in God's arms.

When God embraces our inner child, we may begin to rethink our own treatment of this child. We may find ourselves seating this child at the grown-ups' table. An innocent delight starts spreading into the rest of our life. We'll pause a little longer when we pass by wildflowers in bloom. Maybe we'll dance a little jig to elevator Muzak, not caring so much if our neighbors notice. The path of song extends our laughter and widens our smile. We cry more easily, too. The world will increasingly move us, permeating our senses and nourishing our souls. As we grow to love the child within, we grow to love this precious life, too.

Eventually, on the path of song, we will realize that those manic mystics shlepped to the hills of Tzfat, not only to offer love, but to receive it. Risking foolishness, tasting shame, they unshackled themselves and presented God with the purest of offerings. They received, in return, a love that lifted them clear off the ground. On the path of song, by courageously confronting shame and inhibition, we too can sing to God a new song. We can reunite with our inner child and transform ourselves anew. God will harmonize every note, showering upon us abundant, unequivocal love. Through song, we begin to believe—the God who loves the child within is the God who loves us grown up, too.

THE PATH OF SONG

To embark on the path of song, we need other people. We can meditate alone in the woods. We can stretch by ourselves on the mat. If we hope to offer the song of our souls, we need one another. We need a detailed, intimate accounting of our inhibition, our embarrassment and our shame. These emotions bloom in the presence of others. Singing our hearts out alone in the shower may warm us up, but only by singing with others will we learn to let go.

How do we find fellow singers? We make it easy on ourselves and expand the definition of "song." The path of song may entail an actual song. It may also involve a different medium of artistic and spiritual devotion. We can walk the path of song by bouncing through an African dance class. We can walk the path of song when we bang the drums. We practice our "song" when engaged in any devotional activity that draws us from our shell, presenting us again and again with the choice to play it safe or let go. If a ballroom dance class spins us toward ecstasy, that's our song. If a club's mosh pit propels us from our comfort zone, our fellow headbangers qualify as our gospel choir.

We may find our devotional community within the religious sector. Or we may not. I have sat in synagogues that explode with sound. I have also sat in synagogues that implicitly, or explicitly, forbid release. I have visited churches where parishioners transform their very bodies and breaths into living Halleluyahs. I have also visited churches that suffocate spontaneity. While a community that cherishes decorum may provide a nourishing religious and social environment, it will not serve us on the path of song.

I found my first devotional community at the Arlecchino Theatre Conservatory, a conservatory for the study of theatre, movement, and dance. Arlecchino inhabited a small, brightly colored complex of buildings on the outskirts of the tiny logging town of McCleary, Washington. Redwood-carpeted hills encircled McCleary, the lush green pockmarked here and there from logging clear-cuts. Wildcat Creek rushed from these hills, skirting the town as it wound its way to the Pacific. On my way in and out of town, I frequently spied nude bathers frolicking in the creek, many of them ending their outings with a visit to McCleary's famed Harper Saloon, a perfect dive complete with wall-mounted chainsaw decor.

The lands around McCleary have long served as a haven for Green Party radicals, back-to-the-lander Libertarians, marijuana barons, and devoted Dead Heads awaiting Jerry Garcia's second coming. In 1980, an Italian-born commedia actor joined the mix, migrating west from Chicago. He brought with him a fledgling theatre company of minstrels, jugglers, and clowns, settling his motley crew in McCleary and founding Arlecchino. Ever since, Arlecchino has incubated generations of bright-eyed, barefooted performers, schooling them in the European styles of commedia, melodrama, and clown.

When I arrived in 2000, equally bright-eyed and barefooted, I came ready to launch my avant-garde acting career. While at Vassar College, on the opposite coast, I'd taken countless trips down the Hudson Line, from Poughkeepsie to Manhattan, to see the wildest types of heady theatrical fringe. I loved these untamed creations and admired the risks taken by their eccentric creators. They seemed the last remaining beatniks who'd successfully weathered New York's Giuliani-fication.

I considered joining these free spirits in the belly of the beast, honing my skills Off-Off-Off Broadway and temping to pay the rent. Then Sean, who'd lived in McCleary for years, introduced me to Arlecchino. "Their stuff is crazy!" he told me. "You've got to check them out."

I looked up Arlecchino's website. "We celebrate daring exuberance," boasted its tagline. *Daring exuberance.* Oh boy, that did it. I was looking for just this type of training. I wanted to study the art of letting go, to stand under the lights with nothing to hide. I didn't think of the path of song as soul training. I wasn't aiming for God. I wanted to create honest, authentic works of art. I wanted to blow people's minds. Arlecchino seemed just the place to learn how.

Hardly a week of conservatory classes passed before I received my first memorable lesson in letting go. One of our classes, taught by a spritely Swede who constantly impressed me with her effortless grace and her equal comfort walking on her hands or feet, focused on the mechanics of movement. We learned to get off of our feet, to roll, slide, and tumble our way around the stage. We deconstructed our habitual movement patterns, spending as much time upside down as right-side up. A typical exercise might begin with our teacher's nonchalant direction: "Find an interesting way to cross the stage on just your elbows and your toes."

During one exercise, I found myself paired with a fellow student, Mara, our assignment to explore the dynamics of giving and receiving weight. Our teacher encouraged us to roll different parts of our bodies against one another. "Give over your weight. Explore the sensation of rolling, pressing, lifting," she encouraged. "See where the movements take you. Let go. Have fun!"

Before enrolling at Arlecchino, Mara had been a dancer. She blended a passionate, artistic temperament with lively, sexy irreverence. She glided around the studio in tantalizing black stretch pants, her short-cropped hair sealing the deal. I wanted her. I also recognized that, since she had moved to McCleary with her long-term boyfriend, giving and receiving body weight would comprise the limits of our intimacy.

We began the exercise. Mara's body moved with confidence. I stumbled and strained, living in my head, feeding each bodily sensation into my mind's central processor. I wanted to do well. I wanted to let go. I wanted Mara. These agendas piled up, one on top of the next, cluttering my consciousness. I couldn't focus. I couldn't relax.

"Alright everyone," our teacher called. "Take a moment, thank your partner and give them any feedback you think would be helpful."

Mara and I sat down. Despite my inferior performance, I raised my eyebrows, hoping to receive some encouragement. Mara seemed absorbed in thought. "That was challenging," I offered, "but I felt like we did a nice job of communicating through our bodies." Mara looked up at me. "Ben," she said, "I felt like I just couldn't give my weight to you. I couldn't let go and trust that you would be there."

Ouch. The girl in the stretch pants had called me on my bullshit. It was true. I hadn't let go. I wanted too much. I danced to achieve, to ace the assignment and to impress the teacher. I danced to get the girl. Mara knew. Sensing my inhibition and desire, she couldn't let go. She knew that if she gave me her weight, if she really let go, I wouldn't be there.

The path of song reveals our hidden agendas. We get to know our schemes, the way we transform the act of creation into something self-serving. Many of us begin this path and soon realize that our offering is quid pro quo. We sing and dance for God. But we also want something to feed our ego in return.

To offer God the gift of our song, we need to show up. When we want something for ourselves, however, when we try to impress, to be some version of good and grown up, performance anxiety robs us of presence. Rather than let go, we strategize. We live partly in the present moment and mostly in the next. We've entered the path of song to let go, but here we go again, holding on for dear life.

When we sing with an agenda, we don't just fail to show up. We also get real serious. We clench our body, furrow our brow and suck the air right out of the room. One tool, then, to help us identify this tendency is the presence, or absence, of our smile. As spiritual cross-trainers, we've seen the dark side of determination on the meditation cushion and the yoga mat. We've practiced keeping it light and, in Tony Sanchez's memorable words, "bringing the corners of our mouths to our ears." Now, on the path of song, we turn to the smile once more as diagnostic and remedy. We develop sensitivity to the moments when, head flooded with dreams of greater glory, joy departs. We practice stopping, taking a breath, smiling, and beginning again, this time with lightness in our heart. In this way, our smile provides us an early warning system and a path of return.

Tony wasn't the first teacher to remind me to smile. I learned this lesson years earlier at Arlecchino in another movement class—this one focused on African dance. Our teacher, Justin, a recent Arlecchino graduate himself, began our first class by asking us to form a half-dozen lines on one side of the room. Blasting a CD of African drumming as loud as the speakers could handle, he stepped in front of the lines. With a bright-eyed smile, his lithe, wiry body launched into a choreography of leaps, stomps and twirls. We stared in amazement. His body had become an explosion, his limbs a fireworks display.

"Alright," he turned to us and shouted, "first line, go!"

Bodies plunged forward, attempting to mimic Justin's dance steps in a wave of stumbling, sweat, and self-conscious giggles. Class took us across the dance floor again and again, our hearts pounding with the drums. I absolutely loved it. I loved leaping, arms reaching forward, legs twirling, landing barefoot on the balls of my feet. I felt myself explode with every movement. My body attacked the dance steps with a lion's roar. I felt I could fly.

Justin seemed impressed, giving me little "not bad" nods after I crossed the room. My classmates, too, patted me on the back as we waited in line. "You're an animal out there!" a buddy shouted. Yes. Yes I was.

As we progress on the path of song, we may grow confident. We may imagine that we've arrived somewhere special, that we've gotten somewhere on this mountain climb. The path of song, however, is the territory of the trickster, a monkey howling laughter in the trees. More often than not, the joke is on us.

I learned this the hard way. After a few more sessions of African dance, I had distinguished myself not as the most technically proficient dancer, but as one of a handful who had progressed past novice stumbling. I loved the dance, but I loved this elite status even more. After all, I had come to Arlecchino not simply for education but for confirmation. I wanted to know—was theatre my path? Was I good enough? Did I stand out? Was I—dear God, please make it so—*special?* Every time my line launched forward, I danced to concretize what felt so fragile, ephemeral, and frankly, unbelievable. Could it be? Could it be that I actually belonged on stage? Every turn on the dance floor offered confirmation or rejection. If I exploded with confidence and nailed the steps—yes! I was special! I belonged! If I missed the turn, forgot the steps or noticed that five minutes had elapsed without receiving praise from teacher or peers—oh no! I'd lost my edge! I'd slipped from elite status to mediocrity!

The drumming grew louder, the steps more difficult. I tried my best, but misstepped more and more. *Shit! Come on, Ben, this is your chance. Do it! Do it!*

One morning, near the end of class, as I spun in circles across the floor, I turned to see Justin bouncing next to me. "Ben!" he shouted over the drums. Not sure if he wanted me to stop, I kept my eyes on him but continued to twirl. "Ben!" he repeated, looking me dead in the eyes. "Don't take this so seriously! Smile!" He flashed a wide, toothy grin and bounced away.

Class ended for lunch. Dripping with sweat, T-shirt stuck to my chest and belly, I walked back to my apartment alone. Once there, I entered my bedroom, closed the door and sat down on my mattress. Then I started to cry. *All my life, I've danced this dance.* No matter the medium—academics, theatre, music, meditation—I'd traded the wide-eyed joy of discovery for calculated ambition. What I'd missed! What I'd missed in all this striving—so many moments of joy, of blessing, of gratitude, laughter, and smiles. Sitting on my mattress that afternoon, I realized what I'd done and mourned the lost moments of my life.

On the path of song, we will encounter the tenacity of our agendas. We will try our best to let go and will discover, despite our lofty aims, that a part of us refuses to budge. Justin had invited me: "Don't take this so seriously." I appreciated the invitation. I envied his smile. But old habits die hard. I'd been "taking this seriously" my entire life. "Taking this seriously" had turned me into a straight-A student. "Taking this seriously" had, long ago, buried that hyperactive six-year-old, transforming me from laughingstock to leading man. "Taking this seriously" made me *special.* I yearned to let go. I wanted to smile. But the very thought of living an ordinary life, of not feeling special, left me gasping for air.

That lunch break, while mourning the lost moments, I also lamented these insurmountable odds. How would I ever let go? To sing and dance with joy, to play with daring exuberance, to not take things so seriously would require a fundamental rewiring of my psyche, a reversal of patterns not simply woven into my DNA but practiced each and every day since early childhood. If my ego could take the jubilance of African dance and turn it serious, what spiritual or artistic path stood a chance? I had given myself the gift of a year's immersion in the deep curriculum of letting go. Now, halfway through the year, the curriculum had revealed the man behind the curtain. He imprisoned me.

When that monkey we saw swinging from the trees now clings to our backs, when, though we stamp our feet and shake our fists, that trickster won't shake loose, when we've exhausted all other options, we always have one last weapon left in our arsenal. *Laughter.*

Laughter catapults us sky high. Even if the monkey stays on our back, when we laugh, it starts to laugh, too. Our demons laugh with us as we tumble through space. They haven't let go, but we've let go. We've let go of words like *ego* and *desire.* We've let go of ideas like *spirit* and *path.* We just don't care anymore. In fact, in that miraculous moment when our sobs transform into cackles, it all starts to feel . . . okay. We see that God has served us a big steaming bowl of contradiction, placing in our heart so much love and so much fear. We realize that this tug-of-war in our hearts is not so tragic after all. In fact, it's kind of funny. Hilarious, really.

To laugh in the face of our intractable neuroses takes a monumental exercise of faith. In a face off with our deepest fears, we won't necessarily want to laugh. We may forget that laughter is even an option. The burden of existence will feel that heavy. To prepare for these inevitable moments, I have taken to drawing a smiley face on a notecard and stuffing it into my wallet. During hard times, I take out this quick-reference card, a missive from my saner self. I also carry around a stone of snowflake obsidian, which I picked up at a New Age bookstore in Sedona, Arizona. Snowflake obsidian, a deep black stone polka-dotted with snowflake-shaped splotches of white, supposedly protects one from negative thoughts. Does it really? I don't know. I don't care. When I feel it in my pocket, its presence reminds me to laugh.

Crying in my room after African dance class, I didn't reach for my cue card. I hadn't yet bought my obsidian stone. Instead of laughing, I engaged my default setting—broody and moody. Over the next weeks, I grew somber and isolated, retreating after every rehearsal to my room and my books. McCleary's winter rains set just the right tone. Justin had invited me to lighten up and laugh. I declined the invitation. It seemed just the season for a bit of decadent gloom.

When the world gets too serious, when laughter lies buried beneath frustration and resentment, send in the clowns. Throughout that winter, rumors circulated about our spring unit in clown. Clown class would be taught by Cyrus, a master clown we had yet to meet. "Did you hear?" students would say. "The first moment he meets you, Cyrus will know you. He'll see into your dark places, the places you try to hide, and that's what he'll use to create your clown." The rumors continued: "Cyrus will drive you to your edge. He'll scream at you. He'll fling tennis balls at your head in the middle of a scene if you're not funny. Every year, at least one student drops out of the clown unit altogether. They just can't hack it. The pressure, the work—it drives them mad."

As the clown unit drew closer, the buzz around Cyrus's impending arrival continued to build. A year earlier, I had stood face to face with my revered Zen Master and listened to his condemnation. The last thing I needed was yet another guru, another older man posturing in public with promises of revelation, yet ready, at the first sign of dissention, to denounce and condemn.

While part of me dreaded Cyrus's arrival, I also couldn't wait for him to arrive. A theatrical genius able to see into the depths of my soul? A drill sergeant willing to break all the rules (or at least the rules forbidding teachers from assaulting their students with high-velocity tennis balls)? The year, so far, had familiarized me with the prison of my ego. Did Cyrus possess the key to set me free?

The first morning of clown class, every student, teacher, and administrator in the school clustered against one wall in the main studio space and waited with bated breath. I remember noticing that even the office staff, nontheatrical types who handled things like housing and tuition bills, who had never before attended a studio practice session, sat among us that morning.

Finally, Cyrus entered. He walked casually to the chair that had been placed facing us in the center of the room. Probably in his mid-forties, Cyrus wore jeans and a flannel shirt. His feathered brown hair framed a joyful, energized face. His tiny, piercing eyes scanned the room. Everyone sat silently, face to face with Cyrus, for a good, long while. Then he began to speak.

I don't remember what Cyrus said in his inaugural address. I do remember, however, that in the middle of his talk, he began to speak of the Italian actor who had founded Arlecchino, and who had died a few years earlier. As Cyrus spoke of his mentor, his eyes filled with tears. He began to cry, right there in front of us. Mere mortals might have choked back tears, allowing only a faint shadow of despair to cloud their otherwise cultivated dispositions. Cyrus stood in front of us with an open heart. So open, in fact, that we couldn't help but mourn with him. His fallen teacher, our fallen teacher; his tears, our tears.

Then, in a split second, he transformed again, shifting from tears to wild, cackling laughter as he related a favorite story of the good old days. In response, our company heaved a sigh of relief and laughed right along with him.

My God, I thought. *This is for real.*

"Alright," Cyrus barked, "who's first?"

He moved from his chair on stage to another chair facing the stage. He pointed to the vacated chair center stage and asked the question again.

"Who's first?"

A classmate stood up, walking with rushed strides to the chair, and plopped himself down. The interrogation began. Each of us took a turn in the chair, Cyrus asking us question after question. Following each interview, he asked each of us to stay up on stage and, without explaining why, directed us to perform small, seemingly meaningless activities. Stand up. Sit down. Make a funny face.

He's sizing us up, I thought. In the European clown tradition, one doesn't simply put on a white face, red nose, big shoes and a squirting flower. A clown is not assembled but *uncovered.* The more thoroughly an actor has explored the unkempt essence of his unique, hilarious humanity, the better the clown. Cyrus gave us each a turn in the chair to familiarize himself with our raw material, the material he would spend the next six weeks drawing out and shaping into clowns.

My turn. I walked to the chair. Cyrus asked my name. He asked for additional bits of biography. Then, grinning, he said, "Do this." He opened his mouth, stuck out his tongue and panted like a dog. I opened my mouth, stuck out my tongue and panted like a dog. A few giggles bubbled up from my assembled peers. I giggled, too. Then I waited for my next direction.

"Okay, who's next?" Cyrus said. *Oh. Okay.* I quickly got up and returned to my seat. I didn't get what had just happened, but that didn't seem to matter. The entire morning had felt like a dream. Panting like a dog just added to my general bewilderment.

The following morning, and every morning thereafter, we returned to clown class, to Cyrus's universe. He began each clown class with a few introductory remarks. Then the exercises began. To erode our inhibitions and coax our infant clowns to emerge, Cyrus directed us in an endless series of surreal theatrical scenarios. One morning, for instance, he set up three tables in a row, each one a few feet away from the next. He then split us into groups of four or five. Each group's assignment: climb onto the first table, make our way to the second table, then to the third, and then descend.

Before we began, Cyrus added an important directive: *Be funny.* However we navigated the tables, whatever might happen along the way: *Be funny.*

Trying to be funny is the theatrical version of a Zen riddle. You can't be funny by trying to be funny. You can't think it through, strategizing a hilarious path across the three tables. The audience will sense your effort. They'll taste your desperation. And a desperate actor trying to be funny is just not funny.

Over the course of many mornings, we tried our hardest to earn even a few giggles. We jumped from table to table, or whatever other task Cyrus had concocted that day, pandering in every way possible for a laugh. Over and over again, we failed. Cyrus watched us silently, without even a chuckle.

Then, one morning, Paddy broke through. Paddy wasn't his real name, but from our first day at Arlecchino, he'd introduced himself to his classmates as "Paddy." He stood over six feet tall, with long, stringy black hair, an untrimmed goatee, and a stock wardrobe of goth-style black outfits. Paddy had enrolled in Arlecchino with virtually no acting experience. A juggler by trade, he'd stood on stage plenty of times, but always with balls, pins, and torches circling overhead. From our first day at Arlecchino, I'd watched one teacher after another patiently coax him from his pins, walking him through the theatrical basics of stage presence and vocal projection. He'd grown plenty in the past year, but compared with his more experienced classmates, he still had plenty of catching up to do.

So, on this morning, when Cyrus asked Paddy to take the stage alone and show us his clown, I assumed we'd get a typically mediocre Paddy performance. Paddy began by standing near the back of the stage, eyes downcast and silent. Then, slowly, he started to lumber around. Cyrus called out a few suggestions, similar to an audience shouting scenarios at an improv troupe. Paddy did his best. The rest of us watched, bracing for disaster.

Then I heard it. Laughter. My own laughter. My classmates' laughter. And then, for the first time, the sharp cackle of Cyrus himself. *God help us,* I thought, *Paddy has done it. He's funny!*

Up until now, Paddy's inexperience had proved a hindrance. In clown class, his uncultivated beginner's mind was his greatest asset. He made us laugh because he had nothing to lose. Sure, like any of us, Paddy had plenty of baggage. But he'd spent the year emptying his literal baggage of balls and pins, learning to stand beneath the lights with nothing to hold. Now, hands empty, all that work had paid off. Paddy let go.

Day by day, other classmates joined Paddy, unleashing their clowns to a sound track of Cyrus's guffaws. When Cyrus had first shouted "Be funny!", my classmates had cycled through their usual acting tricks, calling on every fallback solution and clever invention, each performer falling flat. They then picked themselves up and began to break their own habits, performing unpredictably and delighting us with their lack of convention. One by one, I watched each of my classmates risk ridicule. They walked up to the edge, dove off, prepared to die, and that's when we laughed.

Every clown class, I edged toward the cliff, stared down into oblivion, and, overcome with vertigo, backed away. No one laughed. I grew frustrated. How could I risk ridicule for the sake of laughter? I'd spent decades running from six-year-old Ben, from that spastic child bouncing on his teacher's desk, from that impulsive, socially incompetent "before" picture for a Ritalin ad. Could I hand the keys over to that little boy? Would I dare dive over that cliff? I felt trapped. On the one hand, I couldn't risk ridicule by unleashing my clown. On the other hand, if I finished the clown unit without earning more than a single measly giggle, I wouldn't be special. Both options led me smack into my six-year-old self.

I did have a third option, one last Hail Mary. Until now, I'd considered this emergency measure too risky to employ. With the survival of my identity now at stake, however, with Cyrus backing me further and further into a corner, I saw no other option. The time had come. I would channel Andy Kaufman.

I first learned about Andy Kaufman, the actor and performance artist, from the film *Man on the Moon,* which I had seen with my parents a few months before moving to McCleary. I remember seeing this cinematic portrayal of Kaufman's life and then walking around, afterward, as if in a trance. Why had Kaufman's life so captivated me? According to the movie, Kaufman disappeared into the characters he created. He completely disappeared. Kaufman would arrive at his agent's office in full costume, complete with prosthetics. He showed up as Andy Kaufman the actor on talk shows, only to enact shenanigans that would enrage the host and alert security. One of his most famous alter egos, the lounge-singing brute Tony Clifton, showed up to the set of *Taxi* with a prostitute on each arm. When *Taxi*'s producer fired Kaufman the next day, Kaufman had arranged for the press to attend his dismissal.

In Andy Kaufman, I saw the artist I yearned to be. Kaufman had achieved the ultimate act of letting go, erasing all borders between art and life, between the ideal and the real. Kaufman not only performed as his clown. He lived his clown. I dreamed of walking in Kaufman's footsteps, transforming my own life into a never-ending work of art. I longed to live free of social phobias. I fantasized about becoming the crazy-wisdom-Zen-trickster: part poet, part madman, a brilliant beatnik sage. At least in the movie version of his life, Kaufman had achieved the greatest of artistic feats. His act ceased to be an act. This unique approach brought him notoriety and paved his path to Carnegie Hall. Andy Kaufman was *special.*

And Andy Kaufman made us laugh.

I don't remember, during those long mornings of clown class, if I consciously thought of Kaufman. One morning, it just happened. I showed up to clown class as usual. Cyrus invited me on stage for an opening exercise. I performed to a typically quiet house, the absence of laughter as recriminating as ever.

"Stop," Cyrus commanded. He walked onto the stage. Notebooks flew open, hovering pens ready to transcribe the master's every word. Cyrus launched into the finer points of my failure. I listened attentively. Then, suddenly, a simple thought popped into my mind: *Why am I listening as Ben the Actor? I am wearing my red nose. I am still my clown.*

Cyrus continued speaking. I turned away, knelt down and began examining an imaginary flower on the ground. Cyrus paused. "Ben, are you listening?" he asked. I turned back to him, wide-eyed, red-nosed, a child of the moment. My clown didn't understand a word he was saying. My clown didn't understand any of this. Clown class? What did that mean? Cyrus, the stage, the studio, my classmates—all had become the world of the clown.

Then I heard it. A few giggles. And as Cyrus grew more exasperated and my clown grew more obtuse—*laughter. My God*, I thought, *I'm funny! This is it! I've reached my breakthrough!* Channeling Kaufman had worked beautifully. If at first you don't succeed, break the rules of the game. Become your clown—all the time. Turn the world into your stage.

Cyrus asked me to sit down. I felt incredible. Finally, I could take off the dunce cap. I had made them laugh! And not in a scene with my fellow students. On stage with Cyrus himself! Skipping home after class, ringed by McCleary's panorama of redwoods, I wondered if Cyrus saw something in me that day. I had held my own with the master. Did I possess a seed of genius like his own?

Cyrus didn't mention the incident. Classes continued as usual. A few days later, Cyrus sent us in small groups to the costume room, a two-story labyrinth overstuffed with Technicolor jackets, shirts, pants, hats, and shoes. Our assignment was to begin dressing our clown. Our red noses needed an accompanying outfit. We pored through the racks, trying on piece after piece, before returning each to its hanger.

I eventually settled on a skintight black leotard over white tights, and a dark blue, oversized jester's hat. The costume felt simple and audacious. Many of my classmates waddled under layer after layer of linen and wool, their chosen jackets, vests, and scarfs trailing onto the ground as they returned to the studio. In my simple leotard, I felt lithe, sexy, and free. In my jester's hat, I felt wild.

Cyrus noticed the jester's hat right away. As others mingled, showing off their costumes, he walked up to me.

"You can't be a clown with that hat," he said. "That's the hat of the fool. The fool is different from the clown. The fool lives in the world of the clown, but he is not a clown. He is alone. He sees that the clown is crazy. He comments on it. But he can't do anything about it."

Then Cyrus stepped closer, meeting my eyes with his own. "You can play the fool. But you can't wear the red nose if you do."

Yes. There it was. I'd been chosen. I'd been tapped by the master. I wanted to cry. I wanted to shout to the high heavens! *I am special!* I nodded to Cyrus, then took off my red nose. "I'll play the fool," I replied.

Based on Cyrus's description, I acted in our clown exercises as the witness, the outsider, the wise jester surrounded by buffoons. I felt gloriously liberated. Funny? Let the clowns worry about funny. I offered crazy wisdom. Dancing from foot to foot, leotard hugging my body, the bells of my jester's hat jingling, I had been birthed from the surreal struggle of the clown to the prophetic freedom of the fool.

In light of this special status, I began to wonder what Cyrus held in store for me next. I had heard of students in years past quietly tapped for apprenticeships by Arlecchino faculty. Stories of master teachers trailed by their apprentices abounded in the physical theatre world. The director of our school had gotten his start as a student to one such master. Cyrus had, as well. They spoke of their teachers with such love and reverence; clearly, sitting at the guru's feet had transformed them from students to masters themselves. Would I be next?

In addition to the prestige, an apprenticeship might be just what I needed to battle my intransigent ego. Cyrus would scrutinize my every action. He would see my fear disguised as ambition and demand that my true self emerge. As his apprentice, I would place myself daily in the crucible of his direction. If this year at Arlecchino had taught me anything, it had taught me that true art required a daily sacrifice of the ego upon the altar of ferocious play. If I ever wanted to stand upon a stage and offer the truth, I needed the right teacher and the right lifestyle to support this all-consuming mission. An apprenticeship with Cyrus made sense. It felt destined.

I didn't speak to Cyrus about the idea. Not yet. I worried that speaking of an apprenticeship in the middle of our clown training would appear presumptuous. He had made me the fool. I knew that he knew I was special. For now, that was enough.

Still, during class, I took to kneeling on the floor next to Cyrus's chair, a dutiful sidekick ready to obey my master's command. I don't know if Cyrus or anyone else noticed. I didn't care. From this vantage point, kneeling at the feet of the master, classes became electric. Cyrus's every word bore scriptural significance. Each exercise became an opportunity for transcendence. We operated in the world of the clown because, in truth, the world of the clown was more real than the world outside. We entered the surreal within the confines of the stage to arrive at the divine. Cyrus had not arrived in our lives to teach us clown. Cyrus had arrived to liberate our very souls.

As Cyrus's chosen fool, I grew bold. I took risks on stage, twirling and somersaulting, shouldering past the plebeian, red-nosed masses to capture Cyrus's attention. For his part, Cyrus continued to criticize my efforts. *Ah, yes,* I thought, *he is testing me. This is all part of my training.*

Then, one morning, Cyrus set up a particularly challenging scene. Our clowns (and fool) were tasked to perform an improvisational scene alone on stage. Cyrus waited with tennis balls and God knows what else if we failed to delight. When my turn came, I entered the stage literally vibrating with energy. I had grown so excited at this point, so entranced with what I believed to be the arrival of my longed-for destiny, that upon stepping on stage, my body began to shake. I looked at my hands. They wouldn't stop shaking. A moment earlier, while waiting in the wings for my entrance, I had come up with the perfect monologue to recite. Now, to my dismay, I couldn't remember a word. I just stood there, eyes wide, hyperventilating, watching my classmates in the audience looking more and more concerned.

"Not funny. Next!" Cyrus declared.

I didn't move. Instead, I tried to catch my breath. *He's just testing me. I can do this!*

"Still not funny," Cyrus shook his head. "Next!"

"Wait!" I shouted.

Was that my voice? Why was I screaming? What was going on?

"Wait! I can do this!" My voice had reached its highest decibel. "Just give me another chance!"

Suddenly, Cyrus's face contorted into terrifying, menacing fury. He stood up from his chair. "Sit down!" he shouted at the top of his lungs. The force of his voice threw me to the floor. My hands stopped shaking. I sat still and silent.

"I can't control you!" Cyrus bellowed. "Go see Adam! You are not allowed back in my class until you speak to Adam!" With that, Cyrus walked out of the room. Clown class was over.

I saw Adam, the director of our school, the next morning. I entered his office not knowing if I would receive a slap on the wrist or an expulsion from the program. Adam, to my relief, greeted me with a kind smile.

"Tell me what happened," he began.

I told Adam everything. I told him about the jester's hat. I told him about the fool. I described my efforts to embody the fool and my apparent misperception that Cyrus wanted me to push the boundaries of the world of the clown. "I didn't know I was doing anything wrong," I told Adam. "I thought Cyrus wanted me to break the rules."

Adam took this all in for a few moments. Finally, he spoke: "Whether you're a clown or a fool or whatever, Ben, the teacher is the teacher and the student is the student. In clown class, Cyrus is in charge. He makes the rules. That's how it has to work."

I nodded.

"For the rest of the week," Adam continued, "I want you to attend class as an observer. Don't participate in the exercises. Just take notes. Let's see how it goes. If Cyrus says it's okay, you can join back in next week."

I thanked Adam, left his office and headed up to the studio. Clown class had already begun. I snuck in, hoping no one would notice, and sat by the door. A few classmates' heads turned, red noses protruding above sympathetic smiles. Some even came over to put an arm around my shoulders and whisper, "You okay? I was worried about you!" I smiled and nodded.

The following week, Cyrus gave the word to Adam that I could once more join the clowns. I could wear the red nose as we prepared for our final clown project—a student-written clown show on Arlecchino's main stage, attended by locals eager for the free admission and the promise of another Arlecchino wild ride.

If I wanted to succeed in the show, if I wanted to become a clown, if I wanted to be funny, I had to let go. Not by subverting the game. Not with a Kaufmanesque trance or a fool's cap. I would need to let go by releasing my agenda and unleashing my inner child. My awful beautiful inner child. The choice was simple—embrace this child or abandon the red nose for good. I knew what I had to do.

"Excuse me," I said to Cyrus as my classmates packed up at the end of class, "do you have a minute?" Cyrus turned to me. "Cyrus, if it's alright with you, I'd like to continue the rest of clown class as an observer. I think that would be the best thing for me. I'll be here for every class and take notes, but I don't think it's a good idea for me to participate in class or perform in the final show."

Cyrus looked at me unfazed. He seemed to understand. "Okay," he said, giving me a genuinely warm smile. "No problem. Thanks for letting me know."

In the years since Arlecchino, I've spent a lot of time rationalizing and recontextualizing this episode. I've demonized Cyrus, imagining my withdrawal from class as a protest against an emperor with no clothes. I've demonized myself, convinced that my cowardice not only prevented my own learning, but interfered with my classmates' as well.

Now, I see it differently. On the path of song, I simply found my edge. Our heart is a muscle. If we stretch it too hard, too fast, it will contract like other muscles, protecting itself, protecting us. In clown class, I arrived at a landscape I couldn't yet traverse. I arrived at the place where I had to say "no." This very act of saying "no" challenged my self-image. *I can't say "no!" I'm Ben the brave, Ben the brilliant, Ben the spiritual artist and sage.* Yet, in Cyrus's classroom, not ready to expose my inner six-year-old, I said no.

On the path of song, our plan won't always work. We will carefully arrange our ascent up the mountain. Then a storm will blow in, halting our climb. As the wind stings our faces and the rain soaks us to the bone, laughter won't necessarily move us forward. But it will help us heal. It will resuscitate us, reminding us that even from base camp we've got a beautiful view. Just beholding the mountain can be a blessing.

When will our breakthrough come? When will we learn to let go? Who knows? We just keep singing before our infinitely patient Creator, taking our time and going slow. Along the way, it may help to remember this ancient Yiddish proverb: *Der mentsh trakht un Got lakht—Man plans and God laughs.* We had planned to offer God our most beautiful song. Then we fell flat on our faces. But maybe, in the midst of our spiritual collapse, as we repeatedly came up short, we found our clown after all. Maybe our clowns are human beings who try to climb God's mountain, only to roll to the bottom each time, the way we humans do. And maybe . . . just maybe, God finds this pretty damn funny. Maybe God has a laugh for us. Maybe God laughs at all these hapless children, at these wonderful, precious clowns.

THE SUMMIT OF LOVE

Silence takes years to cultivate. Stretching requires decades to refine. Before we even begin the path of song, however, we possess a voice pure and perfect. No need to refine it—our song refines us.

In the Book of Deuteronomy 30:13, Moses reminds us that the wisdom we seek lives within:

> *[The truth] is not in heaven so that you have to ask, "Who will go up to heaven, get it for us and teach it to us so that we can follow it?" And it is not across the sea so that you have to ask, "Who will cross the sea, get it for us and teach it to us so that we can follow it?" The truth is very near, in your mouth and in your heart.*

So it is with song. Whether we imagine ourselves God-seekers or secularists, artistically inclined or creatively bereft, our song lives in us, right here, right now. Even if we wanted to, we could never banish it. Our song presses tenaciously on the inner walls of our heart. It weaves itself amid the maze of our entrails. As we scale heights of neurosis or plumb depths of depression, our song gently hums, never abandoning its post.

We can't banish our song, but we can lock it away. We have the option to silence our song for hours or eons. We may even forget our song exists. Eventually, though, someone will appear to draw it out again. Something will wake us up. We'll walk into a kitchen that smells like the cookies our grandmother baked for us as a child. Or we'll go jogging to an overlook and, though we know we should keep our heart rate up, we'll pause at the breathtaking view. God's grace leaps over our defenses, invades the dormant chambers of our heart, picks every lock, and invites our song to emerge.

At various periods in my life, I've caged my song. God has responded every time with a well-coordinated insurgency. While serving as a rabbi in Boston, for example, my song locked away, God's wake-up call arrived in the form of a question. I was standing in our kitchen, speaking on the phone, when the voice on the other end of the line asked, "Rabbi, what makes your heart sing?"

The question entered my ear, trickled its way down my spine and landed with a thud in my stomach. I stopped nervously pacing and repeated the question to myself: *Rabbi, what makes your heart sing?*

The voice on the other end of the line continued, "What I mean to say is, what part of the job fills you up, makes you feel alive, gives you that sense that this is the right work for you?"

Had someone asked this question a few years earlier, I would have given an elaborate, enthusiastic reply. Then a newly minted rabbi, fresh from seminary and serving as an assistant rabbi in the DC suburb of Fairfax, Virginia, my heart sang as I led prayer services and delivered sermons. My heart sang when teaching classes, counseling congregants, visiting the sick and eulogizing the dead. Sure, some of the work proved a royal pain. I dreaded my once-a-week fumble teaching the Hebrew school's seventh graders. Board and committee meetings left me comatose. The majority of the work, however, felt heaven-sent.

Then we moved to Boston. The Jewish holidays arrived early that year. Before completing my first month as a senior rabbi, I found myself delivering my inaugural sermon before the entire congregation on the morning of Rosh HaShanah, the Jewish New Year. Following the service, congregants descended, eagerly shaking my hand and showering me with praise.

"Home run, Rabbi, home run!"

"Rabbi, that was such a lovely sermon. And your children are just darlings."

"Very nice, Rabbi. Are you going to be joining our Israel Committee meeting this coming Tuesday night? We'd love to speak with you about this year's A.I.P.A.C. conference."

As the reception line grew, I looked over to see Sara surrounded by an equally enthusiastic mob. I could hear congregants asking whether she'd found the Whole Foods, if we liked the preschool, and whether we'd enjoy a noodle kugel brought over for Shabbat.

By midafternoon, we emerged in a daze from the dimly lit synagogue, both of us squinting in the afternoon light. Sara and I walked the few blocks home to our apartment, our two children, then ages six and three, whizzing past us on their scooters.

When we arrived home, Sara distributed rations of challah and honey to our ever-ravenous brood. I, meanwhile, kicked off my dress shoes, threw my jacket and tie on a chair, shuffled up to our bedroom, and belly-flopped onto the mattress. I closed my eyes and nestled my cheek against the cool fabric of the pillow, figuring I'd get a little nap in before we headed off for our next Rosh HaShanah event.

Then, without knowing why, I began to weep. I buried my head in a pillow, hoping Sara and the kids wouldn't hear me, but my sobs only grew louder. Our kids rushed into the room. "Imma," they called to Sara in the same singsong voice they used to report their sibling's infractions, "Abba's crying." I heard Sara walk into the room. "I'm fine," I called, my voice muted by the pillow. "I'm fine. Just give me a minute."

Sara ushered our kids from the room, closing the door behind her. "Abba needs some time alone," I heard her explain as they walked down the hall. "He's very tired. Let's get our scooters and go outside!"

Then, not to God, not to myself, not to anyone or anything really, I heard myself yell, "It's a lie! It's all been a lie!" Anger coursed down my spine. Hands clenched, I pounded the mattress, slamming my fists down again and again until, adrenaline reserves emptied, I turned over on my back and stared up at the white ceiling. I could feel my heart pumping. I could hear my agitated, shallow breath. I closed my eyes. For a long while, I lay there, not really asleep, not really awake, thinking of nothing at all.

Then I picked myself up off the bed, changed my clothes, joined Sara and the kids outside, and pretended like nothing had happened.

A month passed. The congestion of the fall holidays dissipated into a steady stream of regularly scheduled activities. I taught classes, prepared sermons, visited the sick and (sigh) attended board and committee meetings. Sara, meanwhile, found a plum job as the head of admissions for a local Jewish seminary. Our kids grew accustomed to their new surroundings and quickly forgot they'd lived anywhere else.

I might have forgotten the Rosh HaShanah outburst altogether, had it not been for one conspicuous development. I no longer prayed.

My prayer life had begun at the Zen Center in Rhode Island. God had spoken, jump-starting my devotion with a clarion call. In response, I began adding a few minutes of prayer to my morning routine, answering God's voice with my own. I'd forgotten the little Hebrew once learned for my Bar Mitzvah, so I prayed in English from an old summer-camp prayer book.

Later, during my year in Arad, I switched to a traditional prayer book and to an all-Hebrew liturgy. As I chanted each line of liturgy, I cradled the prayer book like a love letter from God. I held the book's thick, soft cover against my palm and felt comforted by its weight. Every dog-eared page felt alive, Hebrew letters shimmering in the morning light.

My mother visited me during this first year in Israel. Together, we traveled to the town of Jaffa, where she purchased a *tallit,* a Jewish prayer shawl, for me at Jaffa's famous Gabrieli Weavers. The following morning, I began my devotions by submerging myself in the *tallit*'s billowing fabric, wrapping the soft cotton around my head and shoulders. From this womb, embraced by the Creator, I could say anything, absolutely anything. "Thank you, God, for bringing my true love Sara to me," I whispered after Sara and I began to date and fall in love. "Thank you, Source of Life, for bringing our sweet children into the world," I added after the births of our son and daughter. At difficult times, I asked God for guidance. When sadness arose, I offered heartache to a God deeply concerned for my every palpitation. God's voice offered no repeat performance. So be it. God would speak when God needed to speak. Until then, I would fill the silence on my own.

Prayer not only served as my communion with God; prayer established my spiritual coordinates, locating my tiny chapter within the great Jewish epic. The prayer book provided a daily dose of Jewish history, its emphasis on God's miraculous salvation. I stood with my ancestors at the Red Sea, helpless, hopeless, Pharaoh's chariots thundering ever close. Then I watched God drown that great army in the watery depths. Filled with awe and wonder, I looked up to the heavens and, together with my tribe, offered a song of thanks. *Who is like You, God, among the gods? Who is like You, so splendid, so holy? You are the Maker of Miracles!* (Ex. 15:11). That three-thousand-year-old story—that was my story. That miraculous Savior—that was my God.

This devotional indoctrination inspired me to structure life around the dictates of Yahweh, the great and glorious Savior. The prayer book reminded me—*Observe the Sabbath day and make it holy* (Ex. 20:8). I stopped driving and turning on and off electricity from Friday at sundown until Saturday's stars emerged. Another verse enjoined: *Do not eat a young goat in its mother's milk* (Deut. 14:21). Sara and I put two sets of dishes on our wedding registry, one for meat meals and one for dairy, forever challenging my mother's organizational skills each time she tried to navigate our kitchen.

Throughout rabbinical school and the beginning of my rabbinate, prayer was the falafel in my pita, the beans in my burrito, supplying a daily medium for connection with God and establishing the foundation for every aspect of my Jewish life. I wasn't a Jew who prayed. I was a Jew *because* I prayed.

Then it stopped. After that first Rosh HaShanah in Boston, I no longer wrapped myself in my *tallit* each morning. I no longer chanted page after page of Hebrew from my well-worn prayer book. I led services at the synagogue, playing my part, chanting and swaying on cue. But I didn't feel a thing.

Why the sudden change? What had happened that Rosh HaShanah morning? What had reduced me to tears and caused me to shout "It's all been a lie!"? What now stood between me and my prayers?

I searched for answers with a therapist. I stretched for answers at my Bikram studio. I consulted a professional coach specializing in Meyers-Briggs personality profiling. I checked out audio recordings by great spiritual sages, listening for answers as I navigated Boston's labyrinth of streets. I even visited a clairvoyant shaman, who channeled reassurances from my deceased grandfather. I stayed hunched over this jigsaw puzzle for the next year and a half, yet my confusion persisted. Every Saturday morning, sitting in a garishly high-backed chair facing the congregation, I mumbled the prayers and wondered: Why don't I feel a thing?

"I think you should write down your story," Sara recommended. "If you want to understand what's happening, start at the beginning and write it all down. See what you find."

So began this book. I wrote about the Zen Center. I wrote about Arlecchino. I logged the moves from Milwaukee to New York to India to Rhode Island to McCleary to Israel to DC to Boston, noting the major spiritual landmarks, each awakening and collapse.

Through writing, I also revisited my decision to become a rabbi. Ten years earlier, as the year at Arlecchino came to a close, I had encountered a crossroads. I could pursue a professional acting career, auditioning, hustling, and searching for opportunities to let my song flow. I'd even outlined a new project—a one-man show to take place on the coastal sand dunes west of McCleary. Out on those dunes, my song would take shape. Out on those dunes, my inner child would run wild.

The closer we came to graduation, the more this plan terrified me. Would I find grant money or would I starve? Even if I secured funding, would anyone show up for performance art in the sand? And even if the one-man show proved a success, what next? Would I flounder, bouncing from job to job and stage to stage, crammed into a closet-sized apartment in New York or LA? I could just picture my parents cringing each time someone asked about me. "Ben's very active in the New York theatre scene," they'd answer with forced smiles. "He's just been cast in an Off-Broadway musical version of *Narcissus and Goldmund* by Hermann Hesse. Have you heard of it? He has a nice supporting role."

I wanted to marry one day and raise a family. How would I do that, sleeping on tour buses and subsisting on ramen noodles? What woman would consent to file jointly, knowing I'd handed over my professional well-being to my six-year-old self? The path of song had begun idyllically amid these beautiful north-coast redwoods, but the path could very well end in poverty, loneliness, or, dear Lord, a part-time job teaching middle school theatre.

I did have another option. The summer before Arlecchino, I had taken a job as a counselor on a teen tour of Israel. A few other sleep-deprived, bleary-eyed counselors and I had spent a month herding a boisterous, hormone-saturated mass of sixteen-year-olds through the Holy Land, from the peaks of the Golan Heights to the shores of the Red Sea.

Our trip had ended in Tel Aviv, where we spent a weekend at a youth hostel just blocks from the beach. The teen-tour organizers required that every participant attend a Sabbath morning prayer service that weekend, a requirement that received groans of disapproval from students eager to sleep in and then hit the beach. I proposed a compromise. If participants didn't want to shlep to synagogue for an early morning service, I would lead services myself. No one exactly cheered at this offer, but the groans dissipated.

Thus, on a steamy Saturday morning in July, I strapped on my guitar and, Pied Piper style, led a congregation of T-shirt and flip-flop clad teens through the streets of Tel Aviv. We arrived at the beach, the landscape already dotted with paddleball players and thong-wearers of the European persuasion. We sat together in a circle. I tuned up my guitar, pulled out a fellow counselor's camp prayer book and started to sing. I'd concocted a service that included a few simple Hebrew songs, poems by Emily Dickinson and the beatnik Lew Welch, and a few prayers from the traditional Sabbath liturgy. I threw in a few tunes from Pete Seeger, Simon and Garfunkel, and Indigo Girls, explaining that "If I Had a Hammer" encapsulated the Jewish ethic of social justice just as eloquently as the classic liturgy. Finally, after one last song in Hebrew, a camp favorite known by all, I wished everyone "Shabbat Shalom."

To my surprise, the group didn't leap up and race away. Instead, most of them milled around, paging through my binder of camp songs or wistfully smiling in the midmorning sun.

"That was really nice," one participant said.

"I wish this was the kind of service we had growing up," another added. "I wouldn't have hated synagogue so much."

"You should be a rabbi," a third chimed in.

A rabbi? Yeah, right. I didn't speak Hebrew. I didn't know a thing about Jewish prayer. My Biblical knowledge ended at the plagues of Egypt. I never went to synagogue and never celebrated holidays. *A rabbi? No thank you.* In a few days, we'd board our El Al flight from Tel Aviv to Newark, I'd make a brief stop in Milwaukee, pack my bags, and then I was off to McCleary.

A year later, as my time at Arlecchino came to a close, as I struggled to find a career more practical than "Sand Dune Performance Artist" or "Actor #4 in Traveling Children's Theatre Company," I thought back to our makeshift service on the Tel Aviv beach. *That was awesome . . . I wish this was the kind of service we had growing up . . . You should be a rabbi.* Was it really so crazy? At the Zen Center in Rhode Island, I had heard God's voice. I had known in my bones—God was, God is, God would always be. I had also realized, in the days and weeks that followed, that I would spend the rest of my life climbing God's holy mountain, listening for the voice and searching for the light. What if I chose a profession where I could bring others with me, a spiritual Sherpa familiar with Sinai's valleys, plateaus and peak?

True, theatre seemed an ideal medium for this mission. A good performance *moves* us. It opens our eyes, holds us breathless and transports us to truth's door. But if the realities of the performer's life terrified me, why couldn't I simply hop from one stage to another? In Tel Aviv, I'd offered my uneducated prayers to the Creator of sand and sea, to the Source of that bright, blue Mediterranean sky. I'd heard a circle of teenage voices join my own. I'd watched eyes fill with wonder. Did their open eyes see any less of God's miraculous creation than the eyes of an audience? Couldn't I accomplish my mission just as effectively on the sanctuary stage?

Sure, I knew next to nothing about Jewish text and tradition. But I could study. I could learn. Then I could take my bag of tricks, my training in theatre and music, combine it with Jewish learning, and package it all into a career that synthesized law and psychology, ethics and counseling, the best of my father the judge and my mother the therapist. Would that be so crazy?

Two roads diverged in a lush green wood. One pointed toward the sand dunes. The other pointed to the rabbinate. And I, I chose the one less traveled by. No, that's not true. I chose the one with better funding.

Following Arlecchino graduation, the twin towers fell, the second intifada raged, and I boarded a flight for Israel. I spent the next year in Arad, immersed in the Hebrew language and spinning every Friday night to Aubrey's song. I also met Sara. Even amid the intifada's violence, Israel became our playground, its cafes and falafel stands—when not exploding—as romantic as any Paris bistro.

The following summer, as we strolled home from a movie at Jerusalem's famed Cinematheque, I asked Sara to marry me. We moved in together, into a fourth floor walk-up in the Jerusalem neighborhood of Katamon. I enrolled in Hebrew Union College, the Reform Movement's seminary, which began its rabbinical curriculum with one year of study in Jerusalem followed by four years in New York. Sara, meanwhile, took the year in Jerusalem to beef up her own Jewish learning, enrolling in a one-year program at the Pardes Institute, a postgraduate school for sacred text study.

Half a world from McCleary, I still walked the path of song. That year in Jerusalem, I wrote Biblically inspired folk songs and performed, for my classmates, a solo, avant-garde retelling of the Book of Jonah. When we moved to New York, however, things began to change. I grew frustrated with Hebrew Union College, which emphasized practical rabbinics and pastoral skills over classical text knowledge. I had enrolled in rabbinical school to answer the call of the head as well as the heart. I wanted to learn how to judge, to flip through the legal codes with ease and to offer knowledgeable, thoughtful opinions on the minutiae of Jewish life. How could I call myself a rabbi if I could barely navigate the writings of my predecessors? How would I guide a Jewish community if I lacked facility in the texts that had, for millennia, held our tribe together?

That spring, I applied for a transfer to the Jewish Theological Seminary, the Conservative Movement's rabbinical school. The Jewish Theological Seminary, or JTS, was located on the Upper West Side in an unfortunate urban netherworld between Columbia University and Harlem. Throughout the nineteenth and twentieth centuries, JTS had housed some of America's greatest Biblical and rabbinic scholars, including heavy hitters like Zecharias Frankel, Solomon Schechter, Saul Lieberman, Mordecai Kaplan, and Abraham Joshua-Heschel. Pictures of these luminaries shaking hands with Truman or marching with Martin Luther King adorned the seminary's hallways, reminding us students that, to quote a rabbinic turn of phrase, we stood on the shoulders of giants.

While Hebrew Union College had focused its curriculum on practical rabbinics, JTS emphasized textual fluency. We rabbis-to-be immersed ourselves, day and night, in the voices of the ancient sages. We read their words aloud to each other, jumping up and down behind our desks as we enthusiastically recited precedent or argued over an interpretation of the text.

Slowly, with the help of our equally enthusiastic, equally devoted professors, my classmates and I transformed. We grew serious and devout. JTS became our boot camp. Our professors sermonized about the epic battles taking place beyond the seminary's walls. Out there, in the sprawl of the American suburbs, Jews were dying by the thousands. Not physically dying, no, but dying spiritually. Each of us, when the time came, would need to parachute into this fray. Armed with our leather-bound books and our memories of Shabbat on the Upper West Side, we would painstakingly turn back the clock and zealously shepherd our flocks back to the fold.

Yes, while Hebrew Union College had prepared us for contemporary pulpits, JTS prepared us for time travel.

Slowly, without even noticing it was happening, I put my song to sleep. With every page of studied text, I exchanged the song of the sages for my own. I'd still take my hyperactive six-year-old out at parties, maybe after a few *l'chaims* with my classmates. The rest of the time, he remained in a cage. I replaced his meandering melody with a thunderous anthem of purpose. No more clown. No more fool. I sang the battle hymn of the great and mighty rabbis.

Following graduation, I took the assistant rabbi position in Fairfax, Virginia. Here, just outside DC's congested beltway, I sang the rabbis' song. It filled me with passion and purpose. I became a holy man doing holy work, and every two weeks, I received a holy paycheck, too. Two years later, the senior rabbinic position opened at a coveted synagogue in suburban Boston. The synagogue advertised itself as a monument to traditional observance amid an eroding religious landscape. It sought an energetic, traditionally minded rabbi to rejuvenate the synagogue's dwindling membership. Applicants should be scholarly yet approachable. A dynamic people person who could captivate the attention of young and old. Musical aptitude a plus. Above all, the congregation needed a prophet to take them up the mountain, to inspire them, to help them fight the good fight and to keep Judaism alive. *Perfect.*

Except that, on that first Rosh HaShanah morning, I stepped fully into the shoes of a senior rabbi and realized I'd made a terrible mistake. I couldn't admit it to myself, not then, not there, not at the beginning of what we all hoped to be a rabbinic tenure of many decades, but I was a fraud. There was no lie. There was only me—the liar. I'd allowed the weight of tradition, the confident conviction of ancient father-figures, to overrule my heart's voice. I had placed my bet on the bearded men of old instead of the heart of a six-year-old boy.

If we hope to climb God's mountain, and all the more so if we aspire to lead others to its peak, we cannot sing anyone's song but our own. We can't let go, opening our heart and soul to the Source of Life, while simultaneously holding tight to a picture of the person we think we should be. God created us just as we are, not as we believe we should be. God waits for *our* offering. God yearns for *our* song. The gates of prayer open to the uncultivated heart, the unrefined gesture, the purest of melodies.

So I stopped praying. Every time I picked up a prayer book, my throat closed. *These aren't my words. This isn't my voice.* The rabbis of ancient Babylonia and medieval Europe assembled this service. They built it to indoctrinate the Children of Israel, to get us on the same page, so to speak. But I didn't want to be on the same page. I didn't want to speak another's words. I didn't want to play a role anymore, not the role of a rabbi, not even the role of a Jew.

It took a good long while before any of this bubbled to consciousness. For that first year in Boston, I pushed forward, hoping that I'd regain my former enthusiasm. Instead, I grew bitter and impatient. At one point, in the midst of morning prayers, I banged the podium and shouted, "Come on! We're standing at Sinai! God waits for us! We can't sit back and wait for it to happen! Join me! JOIN ME!!!" Congregants responded with nervous smiles and a few chuckles. A few voices lifted in volume. After a minute or two, the voices descended again, imperceptible.

I stopped going to weekday prayer services. I skipped committee meetings. The dark halls of the synagogue felt suffocating, so I took as many meetings as I could at Starbucks. Despite this, the congregation wanted me to stay. They wanted to negotiate a new contract. I still ministered to them, still mourned with them through losses, and still danced with them at celebrations. Congregants enjoyed hearing my singing voice at services. Plus, my sermons, sure, they were unconventional, but they weren't boring. I kept folks awake—a bona fide miracle. "He's a little offbeat," congregants would acknowledge, "but he's young. Give him a few years to settle in."

The president of the board spoke to Beth, a fellow board member who worked as a human resources director for a law school. He hoped

Beth could provide some professional coaching, a few one-on-one meetings to smooth out the rookie bumps in the road. Beth took the job, but with our busy schedules, we gave up on face-to-face meetings and instead scheduled a weekly call.

It was on our first call, which I took at home during a lunch break, that Beth asked me that simple, beautiful question: "Rabbi, what makes your heart sing?"

And that did it. Though I cobbled together a feeble reply, and though Beth reassured and reframed, I was done.

A few weeks before the end of the school year, I shared my decision with the board. Together, the board and I drafted a letter to the congregation, an actual letter on actual stationery, which arrived in congregants' mailboxes a few weeks before the summer exodus. The next months were spent on email, phone calls, and coffee dates; hearing from congregants who, understandably shocked, wanted to know what went wrong. I answered them with half-truths. "The pulpit doesn't work with my schedule," I said. "I never see my kids." "The regulars and I want different things—I want to liberalize and they want to rein me in."

Save for a few close family members and friends, I told no one the whole truth. I never said, "I stopped living a lie." I never said, "You remember that first Rosh HaShanah together? When I stood up in front of our congregation and introduced myself? I spent the rest of that day in tears, realizing I'd fooled you all, I'd fooled everyone, especially myself. I was playing a role. I sold you a bill of goods. Sorry. Nothing personal."

After every goodbye, after every coffee date that ended with a congregant shaking his or her head and saying, "Well, Rabbi, we're gonna miss you," I heard two distinct voices in my head. One somber voice decreed: *Ben, you are a horrible person. You've let down your community, your tribe, and your God.* Another voice squealed: *Yippeee! Thank God Almighty! I am free at last!*

Our third and final year in Boston shuffled by. The congregation threw us a goodbye gathering, sans band. Everyone worked hard to smile. I sealed my books into cardboard boxes, reset the passwords on the office desktop and, on my way out, bid farewell to the chapel's brick wall.

Seasoned nomads by this point, Sara and I launched into moving mode, headed for Sara's hometown of Reston, Virginia. Sara's father had passed away the previous year, so rather than buying a home in Reston, we moved into his house. Sara and I took the bedroom that had belonged to her parents before their divorce. Our son took Sara's brother's old room. Our daughter took Sara's. Our kids quickly memorized the two-block route to Sara's mother's house, who rewarded our homecoming with home-cooked meals and, even better, free babysitting.

Seizing this rare opportunity for a professional do-over, Sara traveled to Los Angeles and spent nine weeks training with Bikram Choudhury. I had avoided Bikram's training, my guru issues unresolved. Sara, on the other hand, had never fallen under a teacher's spell. We felt confident in her ability to separate the yoga from the man, to train as a teacher without submitting to the guru. Nine weeks later, having successfully completed the program without incident, she returned a full-fledged Bikram Yoga instructor, shlepping the DC beltway to teach classes from sunup to sundown at half a dozen studios.

Meanwhile, I began searching for work. Leaning on old contacts from my time as an assistant rabbi, I found a smattering of part-time rabbinic work, from chaplaincy assignments to a one-day-a-week rabbi-in-residence at a nearby university. Exulting in my newfound freedom, I went to work with shirt untucked and replaced the tiny skullcap of my past with a thick, crocheted head covering. I barreled down the Dulles Toll Road with windows down, Grateful Dead turned up, always moving, always untouchable.

With Sara teaching around the city, and my work only part-time, I took over a lot of our housekeeping responsibilities. I spent many a weekday morning shopping at Target, the only male shopper in a store filled with mothers, babies, and old ladies. Apparently, the men in this town worked for a living. At 10:30 a.m., they sat at their desks. Though I had my freedom, though I answered to no one, I realized, as I walked Target's wide, fluorescent-lit aisles, that my freedom came at a price. I had gone from guiding a congregation to choosing birthday presents for my children's classmates. I had gone from community leader and spiritual sage to feeling irrelevant and anonymous at Target on a Tuesday.

This feeling of irrelevance and purposelessness was exactly the feeling I had fled when, upon graduating from Arlecchino, I lunged for the rabbinate. Now, the image of myself as lost and lonely, whether dancing upon the dunes or wandering Target on a Tuesday morning, had become reality. A dull throb of shame lodged in my gut. I felt it most acutely when close friends and family visited. They told me they believed in me. They assured me of their support. I wasn't buying it. I could just imagine their conversations: "How sad. He had a great career and a good life in Boston and he threw it all away. When will Ben get it right?"

I needed to forgive myself for ending up on these dunes. I needed to love my inner child, to treasure his chaotic melody, his undeniable dissonance, to hear Ben's song and not feel ashamed. I'd climbed this mountain so many times—in Zen robes, in spandex, in prayer shawl, in leotard, and presently with shirt untucked at Target. God looked through it all, past my outfit, through my skin, down deep to my bones. The Creator waited for my song, my offering, for my imperfect delightful gift. Would I leave God waiting? Would I let the shame of being human once more cage my song?

Shortly after arriving in Reston, the senior rabbi of a large congregation in downtown DC had reached out to me. He'd heard that I'd moved back to town and wanted to know if I'd lead their religious-school services on Sunday mornings. The job was pretty simple, the rabbi explained. A half hour singing with children ages six to eight. A few Jewish songs with guitar, a few simple prayers. No big deal.

I took the gig. I showed up for the first time on a Sunday morning in September, just before Rosh HaShanah. Entering the synagogue's palatial sanctuary, I found a large, boisterous crowd of parents and kids bobbing over seats and weaving through aisles. I plugged in my guitar to the sanctuary's sound system. A violent burst of static and feedback boomed from above. Everyone jumped. "Sorry," I chuckled sheepishly.

The senior rabbi walked up, and though I was meeting him for the first time, he gave me a warm, reassuring hug. "I'm glad you're here," he said with a genuine smile.

"Thanks," I answered. "I'm glad I'm here, too."

I looked out at the crowd. *Shit. I'm nervous. Why the hell am I nervous? This is nothing. It's a random little service for a bunch of kids. I'm a hired gun, a nobody, a schlub in a flannel shirt singing for six-year-olds.*

I hit the first chord. A sea of eyes turned. Voice shaking, I began to sing the opening prayer:

> *Modeh ani l'fanecha, melech chai v'kayam,*
>
> *she-che-chezarta bi-nishmati b'chemla—rabbah emunatecha!*

Every morning for ten years, as I climbed out of bed, I'd offered this prayer. I'd charged into each day with its message in mind:

> *I give thanks to You, living and eternal God,*
>
> *for mercifully returning my soul to me—Your faith is tremendous!*

The senior rabbi had prepped me beforehand, so I knew which tune to use. The children recognized the melody and burst into song.

"Let's get on our feet!" I shouted, bounding down the sanctuary's center aisle, guitar bouncing on my chest. "Let me hear you!"

Kids started spinning each other in the aisles. Parents smiled, some singing, some standing awkwardly with hands in their pockets. I strummed harder. The singing rose in volume. I felt breathless. Looking up to the sanctuary's domed ceiling, I pictured Tzfat's blue sky.

This is meaningless, my head insisted.

My voice answered: "I give thanks to You!"

This is pathetic, my head continued. *A silly service for a bunch of kids.*

The words exploded from my mouth: "Living and eternal God!"

You're thirty-eight years old, for God's sake! And now you're just a party clown! Shame on you Ben! SHAME!

I sang louder still: "You mercifully returned my soul to me!"

All around, kids sang and danced. Beads of sweat trickled down my temples. I hit the final chord. It rang through the sanctuary's speakers. I closed my eyes. We had but one line left to sing.

My heart reached up. It cradled my aching, anxious mind.

"Sing with me," it whispered. "Don't be afraid. Let go."

And then, for one short, sweet moment, I let go.

"Your faith is tremendous! Your faith is tremendous! Your faith is tremendous!"

The song ended. The corners of my mouth reached for my ears. Energy coursed down my spine. The six-, seven-, and eight-year-olds tripped over one another, climbing back to their seats.

"That was beautiful!" I said into the microphone. "So sweet! Okay, now let's get ready for our next prayer."

Our song had just begun.

AFTERWORD

Disclaimer: Spiritual cross-training won't solve all our problems. Spiritual cross-training will not relieve us of suffering, heartache, sickness and death. When we walk the paths of silence, stretch, and song, we still need to watch what we eat. We still say things we regret and have to apologize. We still occasionally stub our toes. We will keep fucking up. Life on planet earth will continue to operate by the unforgiving laws of physics and finance. Good days and bad days just keep on coming.

Fundamentalist dogma teaches us to filter all that we experience and all that we do through a prefab complex of law and lore. On such a path, we need only stick with the program. Once we do so, we're told, things will get better. Spiritual cross-training, by contrast, doesn't operate through promises of salvation. Yes, by walking the path of stretching, I lost forty pounds and my back pain disappeared. By walking the path of silence, I listened less to my demons and more to God's call. Through song, I learned to love myself and to extend that love to others around me.

But I still have problems. I still suffer. I have found no miracle cure.

So why cross-train? Why choose the three-fold mystic's path when this path will not save us from the hurt and heartache of being human? We practice, first and foremost, because *this work makes us kinder.* When we witness our demons in meditation, we extrapolate—other people must be wrestling with demons, too. When we open our mouth to sing and realize that, today, we're just too afraid, we understand that every person on earth grapples with fear. Through cross-training, we connect the dots. We look at our own life and the lives of our brothers and sisters on planet earth and we see undeniably—we're in this fight together.

Spiritual cross-training also allows us to develop a vibrant, authentic and intimate relationship with divinity. Through meditation, yoga, and song, we learn to listen carefully, see clearly, and love courageously. When we open ourselves to creation in this way, we wake up to God's presence in even the most prosaic of moments. Shopping at Target on a Tuesday morning becomes another opportunity to engage the Creator. Not because we're walking through the aisles talking to God (that will frighten the staff), but because we hear and see and feel God's hand everywhere. We don't feel less alone. We *are* less alone.

An everyday relationship with God will not necessarily provide earthly reward. In some arenas of our life, God might not give us what we want. When I go to Starbucks, I ask my favorite barista for just what I want, throwing every imaginable curveball her way. She delivers every time. God's not a barista and there's no Starbucks on the mountain (at least not yet). We cross-train not to develop a transactional relationship with the Source of Life. We cross-train so our friendship with God, our honest, messy, irrational, reassuring, inconvenient, frustrating, sweet, and soulful friendship with God will expand outward and deepen inward. We cross-train because we *need* this friendship. We've been searching for it all our lives.

I am forever grateful to you, my reader, for your valuable time and energy. Thank you for reading these words with an open heart. Writing this book has strengthened my faith not just in God, but in you, in the community of seekers who never stop climbing.

May God bless each of us with courage and patience on our journeys. May we one day reach the summit. And when we do, may we greet each other with smiles, laughter and joyful song.

APPENDIX

The Path of Silence
- Find a quiet place
- Sit, stand or walk with a tall, upright spine
  - If sitting or standing, try to remain as still as possible
- Breathe in and out through the nose
- Bring awareness to the breath
  - Option: Repeat a mantra with each inhalation and exhalation
- When the mind wanders, say to yourself "No Big Deal."
- Smile

The Path of Stretching
- Choose your "stretch"—learn a yoga sequence or another form of mindful movement
- While practicing . . .
  - Move slowly
  - Breathe calmly in and out through the nose

- Pay attention to the spine and initiate all movement from the spine
- Try to align the body with the planes of space
• When encountering pain . . .
  - Pause, Breathe, Relax
  - If and when you feel ready, go a little deeper into the pose
  - If the pain is acute and alarming, back off from the pose
• Smile

The Path of Song
  • Choose your "song"—your form of artistic or devotional expression
  • Find others who practice this type of song
  • While practicing your song with others . . .
    - Notice any agenda you have and let it go
    - Laugh (especially when things don't work out as you hoped)
  • When encountering your edge, the places you can't yet go, be patient and relax
  • Smile

GLOSSARY

Asana

Poses or postures in yoga.

Ashtanga Yoga

A style of yoga founded by K. Pattabhi Jois in the twentieth century.

Bikram Yoga

A system of yoga created by Bikram Choudhury that consists of twenty-six poses performed in a room heated to 105 degrees Fahrenheit.

Feldenkrais

A system of movement and self awareness used to reduce pain and improve physical function. Created by Moshe Feldenkrais.

Hatha Yoga

An ancient system of yoga practice, composed of yogic postures and breathing exercises.

Koan

In Zen Buddhism, a paradoxical question or statement used as a meditation device. For example: What is the sound of one hand clapping?

L'chaim	A Hebrew term meaning "to life." Often used as a celebratory expression.
Rebbe	A Jewish spiritual leader or teacher.
Savasana	A yogic pose (often referred to as the Corpse Pose) in which the practitioner lies on his or her back with arms and legs outstretched and relaxed.
Shabbat Shalom	A Hebrew term meaning "May you have a peaceful Sabbath."
Shamatha-Vipassana	A combination of meditative terms meaning tranquility and insight, respectively. Also a style of Buddhist meditation focused upon the breath.
Shanti	A term most commonly meaning peace. Often used as a chant in yogic meditation.
Tadasana	A yogic pose (sometimes referred to as Tree Pose) in which the practitioner balances on one leg with the opposite foot held in front of the hips.
Yarmulke	A Jewish head covering.

ACKNOWLEDGMENTS

The ancient sage Rabbi Yehoshua ben Perachiya advised: *Find for yourself a teacher and make for yourself a friend.* I give thanks to wise teachers turned friends and trusted friends turned teachers—all of whom helped to birth this book.

Thank you to my agent, to the savvy and soulful Priya Doraswamy at Lotus Lane Literary. Thank you to Erin Mooney and Sarah Faulkner, my energetic and insightful editors, and thank you to the entire Grand Harbor Press team. Thank you David Goldberg for your counsel, Rachel Litcofsky for your PR skills and Eric Kemp for your expert eye. Thank you Alex Boyar, Judith Rosenbaum, Anita Diamant and Adam Harmon for helping me navigate the wilderness of publishing. And, of course, thank you to the crew at the Plaza America Starbucks in Reston. You let me nestle in my corner and kept the decaf warm.

Thank you to those who taught me silence: Tony Somlai, Linda Somlai, Mathew Somlai, Ken Kessel, Cate Pfeifer, Zen Master Wu Kwang, Zen Master Dae Kwang, E.H. Rick Jarow, the Original Root Zen Center sangha and the Great Lake Zen Center sangha.

Thank you to those who taught me to stretch: Marlene Gryesten, Jennifer Goldstein, Kelly Mara, Julie Sanders, Morgan Eash, Cynthia Gramer, Bob Meade, Gerdette Armour, Jenny McParland, Jon Kjellman, Diane Ducharme, the Pure Om Fairfax crew, the Bikram Reston crew and the Bikram Tysons crew. Thank you above all to Tony Sanchez, Sandy Wong-Sanchez, Jerome Armstrong and the December 2013 Yogic Physical Culture Academy graduating class—you inspired me to bend with a clear mind and a light heart. And thank you Benjamin Lorr for writing one of the best books on yoga I've ever read.

Thank you to my teachers of song: Mary Ellen Meyer, Barbara Gensler, Jack Forbes Wilson, Alexa Scott-Flaherty, Saul Kaiserman, Daniel Stein, and Rabbi Aubrey Isaacs. Thank you to my theatre conservatory faculty and to the conservatory graduating class of 2001—you watched me go insane and you didn't seem to mind.

Thank you to my friends and teachers in the rabbinical trenches who continue to inspire me, hire me and keep me connected. Thank you Rabbi Gil Steinlauf, Rabbi Lauren Holtzblatt, Rabbi Sarah Tasman, Rabbi Shira Stutman, Rabbi Leila Berner, Rabbi Sid Schwarz, Rabbi Matisyahu Tonti and Rabbi Jordan Bendat-Appell. Thank you Michal Shuldman and Rabbi Randy Fleisher for teaching me how to pray. Thank you Karen Pemstein Deresiewicz for asking the right question at the right time. Thank you Father Vasily Lickwar for listening to a lost sheep and pointing him home. Thank you Rabbi Greg Litcofsky, Rabbi Scott Perlo, Rabbi Aaron Philmus and Rabbi Leor Sinai—your friendship is a blessing.

I give thanks and bow to my *rebbes,* to the spiritual giants who have opened my heart and nourished my soul. Thank you Robert M. Pirsig, Jiddu Krishnamurti, Pema Chödrön, John O'Donohue, B.K.S. Iyengar, Reb Zalman Schachter-Shalomi and Thich Nhat Hanh.

Thank you to my family. Thank you Sean Armstrong, Ben Toth and Norman Lasca. You are brothers in all but blood. Thank you Michael Schudson for your steady encouragement and sage advice. Thank you

Judy Barokas for your expert editing eye and for all the warm meals and free childcare. Thank you Ben and Sara Barokas for sheltering us from the storm and helping us build a new life on home turf. Thank you Zoe Florence for your artful eye and unwavering support. Thank you Joel Schudson for your love—steady and true—and for your song, which brought me home to my own. Thank you Karen and Charlie Schudson for your boundless love, for cheering me on through every chapter and for insisting that I follow my heart, try my best, help others, and have fun. Thank you Lev and Avital. You are the gurus for whom I've always searched and you show me the way, every day, back to my heart. Thank you Sara—you are my home.

Last but definitely not least, I give thanks to the Creator, the Source of Life, for calling me to the mountain and for restoring my soul.

ABOUT THE AUTHOR

Benjamin Shalva was born in Milwaukee, Wisconsin, attended Vassar College and received rabbinical ordination from the Jewish Theological Seminary. His writing has been published in *The Washington Post*, *Elephant Journal* and *Spirituality & Health Magazine*. In addition to writing, Ben works as a freelance rabbi, yoga instructor, meditation teacher and song leader, teaching Spiritual Cross-Training seminars and workshops nationally and internationally. He serves on the rabbinic faculty of the Jewish Mindfulness Center of Washington and the 6th & I Historic Synagogue in Washington DC, and leads musical prayer services for Adas Israel Congregation in Washington DC and for Bet Mishpachah— Washington DC's LGBTQ Jewish congregation. He also serves as the Camp Rabbi and Director of Jewish Programming for Tamarack Camps in Ortonville, Michigan. Ben lives in Reston, Virginia with his wife Sara and their children, Lev and Avital.